Tungsten

From Juan Larrea, *Al Amor de Vallejo* (Valencia, Spain: Pre-Textos, 1980). Photograph by Juan Larrea.

Tungsten

a novel by

CÉSAR VALLEJO

Translated by
Robert Mezey

with a Foreword by
Kevin J. O'Connor

SYRACUSE UNIVERSITY PRESS

Translation © 1988 by Robert Mezey

First published 1988

97 96 95 94 93 92 91 90 89 88   5 4 3 2 1

The paper used in this publication meets the minimum requirements of
American National Standard of Information Sciences—Permanence of
Paper for Printed Library Materials, ANSI Z39.48–1984. ∞™

Library of Congress Cataloging-in-Publication Data

Vallejo, César, 1892–1938.
   [Tungsteno. English]
   Tungsten : a novel / by César Vallejo ; translated by Robert Mezey
; with a foreword by Kevin J. O'Connor.
     p.   cm.
   Translation of: El Tungsteno.
   ISBN 0-8156-0226-X (alk. paper)
   I. Title.
PQ8497.V35T813   1988
863   dc19   88-19996
                                          CIP

Manufactured in the United States of America

This translation is
dedicated to
my old friends
Ronald Goodman and Alan Trachtenberg

Robert Mezey is Professor of English and Poet-in-Residence at Pomona College. He is the author of many books and has received the Lamont Poetry Award, the Robert Frost Prize, Ingram Merrill, Guggenheim, and National Endowment for the Arts fellowships, and a poetry award from the American Academy and Institute of Arts and Letters.

Kevin J. O'Connor is Assistant Professor of English at Colorado College.

Contents

Foreword

Kevin J. O'Connor

Vallejo is now a common ground in our literature, a type of degree zero of the cultural object, a place at once empty yet eternally open to signification. —Enrique Ballón Aguirre

César Vallejo's fame as a poet has spread far beyond the boundaries of the Spanish-speaking world. The Eshleman/Barcia translation of his posthumous poetry became the first volume of translated verse ever to win the National Book Award. The dazzling technical innovations of the early vanguard poetry, *Trilce*, and the anguished expressiveness of the poetic structures Vallejo stressed almost to the breaking point in the final *Poemas humanos* have established him, without question, as one of the greatest poets of our age.

But the figure of the vanguard poet has obscured Vallejo's other dimension as proletarian novelist and playwright. Ironically, while much of the poetry for which Vallejo has become justly famous lay unpublished until his death, the proletarian novel *Tungsten* was as great a success as Vallejo would know in his lifetime. Yet the novel, which became a best-seller after its

ix

publication by Editorial Cenit in Madrid in 1931, only now appears in English, fifty years after his death.

"How different it is for us now!" Chilean novelist Antonio Skármeta remarked in a recent conversation, noting that the English translation of his own novel *Burning Patience*, based on the last years of Vallejo's contemporary, Pablo Neruda, appeared within a year of the original Spanish edition.

The reasons for this long delay in the appearance of the English edition of *Tungsten* are quite different from those which caused certain works by Vallejo's North American contemporaries, Hemingway and Fitzgerald, to come to light only recently. The narrative fragments and manuscripts which these authors, in some cases deliberately, left unpublished reach today's reader with the authority of established genius in a market confident of their value.

Tungsten, on the other hand, despite its early commercial success, has been banished from the canon of contemporary Latin American literature as a proletarian novel (which it is) and a lamentably anomalous narrative detour in the development of a poetic genius (which, we would argue, it is not). That Vallejo, the poet whose brilliant and provocative verse still challenges the reader, would decide to craft a novel of socialist revolution has caused no little consternation among his critics.

Juan Larrea, for example, even argued for a time that the period of Marxist militancy during which *Tungsten* was written was one in which Vallejo had abandoned the writing of poetry altogether, as though the writing of his poetry—even today perhaps the most daring vanguard work ever produced in Latin America—were somehow contingent upon Vallejo's

proximity to the political mainstream. Though we now know
that Vallejo did continue to write poetry at the time he was at
work on the novel, for some the critical judgment abides: in
Tungsten the lofty aesthetic standards of Vallejo's poetry were
compromised in the service of a Marxist thesis.

But if we are to understand Vallejo's development as an
artist and human being capable of producing the final *Poemas
humanos*, a more organic view of the novel's place in his writing
may be needed. There is no question that the period of 1929–
31 was one of profound anxiety and uncertainty in Vallejo's
own life and in the lives of millions in Europe. He had arrived
in Paris in 1923, following the trajectory of Latin American
writers begun, as the late Angel Rama observed, in 1828 with
the Argentine Luis Echeverría and continuing to the present
with such contemporary masters as Fuentes, Carpentier, and
Cortázar. The appeal of Paris as the cultural crucible of the
West also attracted Vallejo, but the poverty he experienced in
the early years and the misery he observed during the Depression led him to comment caustically: "C'est Paris, reine du
monde! C'est Paris, mort de la mort!"

Eventually Vallejo, like other Latin American intellectuals
before and after him (Rubén Darío and Julio Cortázar), was
able to secure a respectable living doing newspaper work, in
this case cultural commentaries on the Parisian postwar scene
which appeared in several Latin American publications, including *Mundial, Comercio,* and *Variedades.* By 1928, Vallejo
had also found regular employment in the offices of *Les Grands
Journeaux Ibéroamericains.*

Everything fascinated him—Stravinsky, Picasso, Chaplin,
Freud, Spengler—and his reports reveal the sophisticated, cos-

mopolitan sensibility of an acute observer capable of experiencing and integrating the extraordinarily diffuse and often disturbing cultural movements of the time: from surrealism to psychoanalysis, from Lenin to Schoenberg. Living in Paris, Vallejo was keenly aware of the continuing impact of the Great War, as well as the presence of Marx's "spectre" recently embodied in the Bolshevik Revolution. But, as Tulio Halperín Donghi has pointed out, the most disturbing event for Latin American intellectuals, the one which showed more than any other, just how fragile was this European world into which they hoped to become integrated, would be the Crash of 1929.[1]

Vallejo's newspaper articles enabled him to survive in the French capital. But in 1928, he began to express frustration at his inability to work seriously on his own writing while leading the fragmented life of the cultural columnist: "Almost five years have gone by in Paris. Five years of waiting, being able to undertake nothing serious, nothing tranquil, nothing definitive, and troubled constantly by a financial fear which allows me to begin or deal with nothing in depth. Is there anything more horrible?"[2]

He had written a novella in Paris on the Inca empire, *Toward the Kingdom of the Sciris*, which he had been unable to publish, but otherwise nothing. He talked of going to New York or of returning to Peru, but when the Peruvian consulate provided money for the passage back to Callao in 1928, Vallejo instead used the money to travel to Moscow.

His three trips to the Soviet Union (1928, 1929, and 1931) provoked a dramatic change in the poet. An account of his experiences, *Rusia en 1931*, published in Madrid by Ulises, was second in sales only to the Spanish translation of Remarque's *All Quiet on the Western Front*.[3] In December 1930, Vallejo was expelled from France by the Direction de la Sureté Générale for his Marxist activities (among them participation in protests and membership in the Parisian cell of the Peruvian Socialist Party, a Marxist-Leninist group founded in 1928). Vallejo traveled to Madrid with his wife, Georgette, a French citizen whom he had met in Paris and with whom he would live until his death. There, with the help of Spanish poets Gerardo Diego and José Bergamín, he was able to publish the first Spanish edition of the vanguard poetry *Trilce*, which originally appeared in Peru in 1922. But despite Lorca's personal intervention on his behalf (with Camila Quiroga, among others), Vallejo's attempts to have his dramatic works staged in the Spanish capital ended in failure. None of his plays, including *Colacho hermanos*, a theatrical version on the theme of *Tungsten*, would be produced during his lifetime. The stories likewise remained unpublished. "Paco Yunque," the moving portrait of the Indian whipping boy of an American industrialist's son, clearly suggestive of W. R. Grace, was considered "too sad" for European audiences by the editor who reviewed and rejected the manuscript. In a 1932 letter to Gerardo Diego, Vallejo asks, "What's the point of writing if there are no publishers? There's nothing left to do but write and keep the manuscripts under lock and key."

Tungsten, then, becomes Vallejo's first published volume of work written after leaving Peru. The raw, searing outrage of the novel, coupled with the spare quality of the prose, are in striking contrast to the literary virtuosity, the sheer dynamism of language in *Trilce*. This would appear to lend some credence to the critics who see little in the novel beyond a sloganeering call for socialist revolution. There are many reasons, however—evident here in Robert Mezey's carefully controlled rendering of Vallejo's words—why this would appear to be a less than adequate appraisal of the work.

First of all, Vallejo himself was too sophisticated a literary mind—as his newspaper articles and unpublished literary theory reveal—to attempt a facile fusion of form and dogma. Indeed, shortly before his first trip to the USSR, he had written persuasively of the need for freedom of artistic expression, a freedom beyond the constraints imposed by any party platform or program:

> When Haya de la Torre [founder of APRA, the American Popular Revolutionary Alliance] underlines for me the need for artists to assist revolutionary propaganda in America with their work, I say to him again that in my capacity as a man I find his demand a great political undertaking, and I sympathize sincerely with it. But in my capacity as artist I accept no order or proposition, mine or anyone else's, which, however well intentioned, subjects my aesthetic freedom to this or that political propaganda.[4]

Upon his return from the Soviet Union, however, Vallejo challenges the notion that the writer or artist may exist in society "*au dessus de la melée*". He argues that if artists like Picasso (and, clearly, Vallejo was referring to the pre-*Guernica* Picasso) do not get involved in politics, it is for one reason only: fear of reprisals. According to Vallejo, these opportunistic artists know nothing of Zola's dictum, "I cannot be silent, because I don't want to be an accomplice."

While there is an unmistakable resonance even in the novel's title (*Tungsten*) of the revolutionary literature emerging at the time in the USSR (think of Gladkov's *Cement* or Ostrovsky's *How the Steel was Tempered*), Vallejo's determination to write an *engagé* novel cannot really be considered a departure from previous literary tradition in Latin America. From the time of the Conquest, writing on the continent had been deeply immersed in the social. From the *Crónicas* and accounts of the destruction of the pre-European civilizations, to the nineteenth century indictments of the oppression of the gaucho (José Hernández' *Martín Fierro*) and the Indian (Clorinda Matto de Turner's *Aves sin nido*), the writer had been a force for challenging the established order. In fact, this tradition continues strongly in the writings and public statements of many contemporary Latin American writers, including the Nobel laureates Pablo Neruda, Miguel Angel Asturias, and Gabriel García Márquez. Consider García Márquez's chronicles of Vietnam and Angola, Nicolás Guillén's elegy on the death of "Che Comandante," the tragic deaths of the young contemporary revolutionary poets Roque Dalton, Javier Heraud, and Otto René Castillo, and the "disappeared" Argentine writers Rodolfo Walsh and Haroldo Conti.

There is no remote Parnassus for Latin American writers, and it appears that, whatever their own intentions, their words inevitably resurface in the landscape of their own societies. "Poetry belongs to the one who uses it, not the one who writes it," the postman tells Neruda in Skármeta's *Burning Patience*.

Whether it is Vargas Llosa opposing the nationalization of Peru's banks, or Cortázar protesting U.S. troop movements along the Honduran border with Nicaragua, whether it is

Borges accepting the homage of Pinochet or Neruda running as a presidential candidate, writers are found in the
tissue of society and their words are the cells of its own self-
knowledge.

Mario Vargas Llosa, perhaps the best-known living Peruvian writer, once shared a visioɩ of the writer's responsibility
to work for social justice. Upon receiving the Rómulo Gallegos
Prize for his novel *The Green House*, Vargas Llosa proclaimed:

> Literature may die, but it will never be conformist. . . .
> The reality of [Latin] America offers the writer a whole
> panoply of reasons to be a dissident, to live as a mal-
> content. . . . Societies where injustice is law . . . our tur-
> bulent lands provide us bountiful, exemplary materials to
> show in fiction, directly or indirectly, through facts, dreams,
> testimony, allegory, nightmares or visions that there is
> something wrong with reality, that life must change.[5]

Lamentably, the reversal of Vargas Llosa's earlier social
commitment has led, some would say inevitably, to his de-
fense of the rights of Peruvian banks. And one is reminded of
Fredric Jameson's formulation: "It is not only political history
which those who ignore are condemned to repeat . . . the
older controversies rise up to haunt those who thought we
could now go on to something else and leave the past behind
us."[6]

Those who rejoiced at the APRA victory in the presidential elections of 1985 are now left to confront the Lurigancho
prison massacre ordered by Alan García. The apologies of-

fered by one Peruvian official ("You also had a massacre") do
not ease the anxiety of those who believed that García represented something other than Nelson Rockefeller's Attica when
he became the first successful Aprista presidential candidate in
the party's history. Arguments about the need to respond
forcefully to the threats posed by the Marxist guerrilla movement, Sendero Luminoso, only make more poignant the call
of *Tungsten's* protagonist, Servando Huanca, to the victims of
the Quivilca mines. Now, fifty years after Vallejo's death, the
"Shining Path" of Vallejo's contemporary, José Carlos Mariáte-
gui, controls the departments of Ayacucho and Junín, in the
sierra whose injustice Vallejo had witnessed as a child and
denounced as a writer.

Tungsten's indictment of the abuse of the Indians of the
sierra pressed into mining service fits well within the tradition
of Latin American protest literature. Even in the opening
poem of the vanguard *Trilce*, Vallejo had focused on the mate-
rial phenomenon of Peru's major nineteenth-century export
commodity, guano. In the novel, though, the vantage point of
his exile and recent experiences in the Soviet Union add a new
dimension to Vallejo's understanding of exploitation in his native Peru. The tungsten, with its continuing price of blood-
shed and misery, is destined for the U.S. entry into the Great
War in Europe. That conflagration, with its ten million dead
was, as Paul Fussell has written in *The Great War and Modern
Memory*, "too much for literature to bear."

Interestingly enough, Vallejo uses one of Fussell's key images of the impact of that war on modern consciousness—the
"trenches"—in discussing the new forms required of revolutionary art. In the impressionistic, staccato style Vallejo uses in

his notebook reflections on the problems of revolutionary art, he says the form of that art must be "the most, simple, direct and bare-boned possible. An implacable realism. Minimal elaboration. The emotion must be looked for by the shortest route and at point-blank range. Art of the foreground. Phobia of half light and nuance. Everything raw—angles not curves, but heavy, barbaric, brutal, as in the trenches."[7]

Vallejo was aware of the horrors experienced by the Peruvian poor long before he left for Paris. Like the protagonist of *Tungsten*, the Indian ironworker Servando Huanco, he too had observed the abuses of the sugar plantation. Like Leónidas Benites, the bookkeeper anguishing over his role in the exploitation, Vallejo's plan to earn money to attend the university had made him witness (and accomplice?) to the brutalization of the workers at the Larco family's Hacienda Roma in 1912. Angel Flores tells us that the scenes of oppression Vallejo sets in "Quivilca" are, in part at least, an evocation of the events he had witnessed in 1913 in Quiruvilca. It should also be remembered that, in the aftermath of a violent incident in Santiago de Chuco that had left the most important warehouse in the province in ashes, Vallejo spent four months in prison, until the protests of his friends and admirers led to his release in February of 1921. Vallejo's identification with the Indians of the sierra ran much deeper than sympathy alone. Both his grandmothers were Chimú Indians. Both his grandfathers were Spanish priests. Vallejo's sharply drawn Indian features led to the familiar nickname *cholo* (or *mestizo*), which his friends always used. His childhood spent in the remote sierra of Santiago de Chuco, three days by horse from the nearest train station, left him with a vision markedly different from that of the Lima criollo.

Now, Vallejo sees these Indians and the miserable unem-
ployed masses of Depression Paris (whom he will later evoke
in the Whitmanesque *"Parado en una piedra"*) as victims of the
same monstrous force. In the climactic closing pages of *Tungsten*, there is an almost religious tribute to Lenin, of whom,
Vallejo tells us in an obvious reference to the destruction of
Diego Rivera's Rockefeller Center mural, "the bosses cannot
even stand to see a picture" (*"no le pueden ver ni pintado"*). It is
Lenin's formulation of the roots of the war, and his vision of
the inevitable triumph of the oppressed as a result, that seem
to resound in Vallejo's often searing description of the abuses
of the mining officials.

> The tens of millions of dead and maimed left by the War—a
> war to decide whether the British or German group of fi-
> nancial marauders is to receive the most booty— . . . are
> with unprecedented rapidity opening the eyes of the mil-
> lions and tens of millions of people who are downtrodden,
> oppressed, deceived and duped by the bourgeoisie. Thus,
> out of the universal ruin caused by the war a world-wide
> revolutionary crisis is arising which, however prolonged and
> arduous its stages may be, cannot end otherwise than in a
> proletarian revolution and in its victory.[8]

The sense of hastily drawn fragments which the reader
experiences at times in the novel can perhaps be recognized
as Vallejo's desperate urgency to communicate his understanding of the cause of the horrors of World War and Depression,
an understanding he has gained only after experiencing the
three worlds (dependent, imperialist, and socialist). Vallejo

seems to be responding with the "language of the trenches" to the urgency of Lenin's call to end the trenches, believing this will end injustice and hasten the ultimate and inevitable victory.

Vallejo's vision always remained more utopian than apocalyptic. The end result of the struggle for Vallejo would be the "universal embrace of love," even though there might be a preliminary phase of revolutionary violence. But, despite his political awakening, Vallejo continued to judge harshly the schematized writing of the "party hack" and reserved his greatest scorn for the "parrots of *Capital*" who, "in order to decide whether to laugh or cry at a passerby who slips on the street, take *Capital* out of their pockets and consult it."[9]

The appeal of Marxism was perhaps more emotional than theoretical for one who, as he said of himself, had always lived "underneath the bourgeois banquet table." And he suggested that if revolutions did begin with the "pariah's cholera," then the revolutionaries of the day had a willing participant in him. But Vallejo's enthusiasm for the role of revolutionary writer, despite his earlier reservations about becoming a tool for political programs, may be understood as a breakthrough in his understanding of the events of the war and the Depression through the totalizing vision of Marxism-Leninism. As Lukács has noted: "It is perfectly possible for someone to describe the essentials of an historical event and yet be in the dark about the real nature of that event and of its function in the historical totality: i.e., without understanding it as part of a unified historical process."[10]

Now, however, Vallejo's Marxism enables him to see the injustices he has witnessed and been a victim of as part of the

same process, and he works frenziedly to share this vision
with those whose understanding will lead to the system's destruction. When Vallejo denounces the abuse of the Indians in
the tungsten mines, he does so with the vision of the libera-
tion of "Indians everywhere," from Bolivia and Peru to China,
India, and Russia.

Even with this commitment, however, Vallejo was not prepared to accept that the revolution required the sacrifice of the
writer's artistic freedom and responsibility, and just as he ridi-
culed those who needed to consult Marx to know whether to
laugh or cry, Vallejo had little interest in or respect for those
who believed that by spouting phrases about dialectics one
was producing socialist literature. Socialism ran much deeper
for Vallejo:

> The socialist poet does not reduce his socialism to themes
> or poetic technique. He does not reduce it to the introduc-
> tion of fashionable phrases of dialectic or marxist
> rights. . . . The socialist poet assumes, instead, an organic
> and tacitly socialist sensibility. Only a man who is *tempera-*
> *mentally* socialist, whose public and private conduct, whose
> way of looking at a star, of understanding the rotation of the
> wheel of a cart, of feeling pain, of performing an arithmetic
> operation, of lifting a stone, of keeping silent or of mending
> a friendship are organically socialist, only that man can cre-
> ate an authentically socialist poem.[11]

Is Vallejo's novel worth reading? Certainly the intensity of
the images of oppression are as gripping as the reader may

expect to find in a continent which, as Vargas Llosa pointed
out, is full of examples of injustice. Is the spare, fable-like
quality of the opening passage mere socialist realism? Or is it
now possible to see the novel's apparently unmediated realism
as one level of literary discourse? And may not Vallejo's mixing
of the different levels of discourse—the language of the sierra,
the telegram discussing the government massacre—have much
to do with Bakhtin's vision of the novel's intertextuality? Could
Vallejo's vision (rooted in his own past) of the Indian's innocence, of the Indian's inability to comprehend the fundamen-
tal nature of the labor exchange, heighten via a Brechtian
Verfremdung the awareness of the horror of the discarded
worker on the streets of Depression Paris?

One may say of Vallejo what Alfonso Sastre has said of
Lorca: that he did not live long enough (he was forty-six years
old at the time of his death) to develop the mastery of another
genre besides poetry. But there is no question that this *is*
Vallejo, that he is here in these pages as much as in the posthumous poetry and his plea for the Spanish Republic, *Spain,
Take This Cup From Me*. It may be a final confirmation of
Vallejo's faith in the word, the faith which enabled him to go
on writing for an audience which might never be found, that,
fifty years after his death, his words will find resonance for the
first time in another part of a world that for him was one.

And just as, at the novel's close, the dizzying, exhilarating
flood of revolutionary words filling the timekeeper's head and
keeping him from sleep ends finally with the shedding of
tears, Vallejo may yet triumph by sharing his vision and having
us feel both the enormity of the crime and the dream that will
end it.

Notes

1. Angel Rama, *La novela en América Latina: Panoramas, 1920–80* (Colombia: Instituto Colombiano de Cultura, 1982), 136.

2. *114 Cartas de César Vallejo a Pablo Abril de Vivero* (Lima: Juan Mejía Baca, 1975), 82–83.

3. Georgette de Vallejo, *Vallejo: allá ellos, allá ellos, allá ellos!* (Lima? Zalvac, 1978), 51.

4. Angel Flores, ed. *Aproximaciones a César Vallejo* (New York: Las Américas, 1971), 92.

5. Adolfo Prieto, "Conflicts de generaciones" in *América Latina en su Literatura*, ed. César Fernández Moreno (Mexico City, D.F.: Siglo XXI, 1972), 414.

6. Fredric Jameson, Afterword, in *Esthetics and Politics: Debates between Ernst Bloch, Georg Lukács, Bertold Brecht, Walter Benjamin and Theodor Adorno* (London: NLB, 1977), 196.

7. César Vallejo, *El arte y la revolución* (Lima: Mosca Azul Editores, 1973), 123–24.

8. Vladimir Ilich Lenin, *Imperialism: The Highest Stage of Capitalism* (Peking: Foreign Languages Press, 1975), 6.

9. Vallejo, *El arte y la revolución*, 91.

10. Georg Lukács, *History and Class Consciousness*, trans. Rodney Livingstone (Cambridge, Mass.: MIT Press, 1971), 12.

11. Vallejo, *El arte y la revolución*, 28.

Translator's Preface

I began to translate *El Tungsteno* in Barcelona in the early winter of 1972, at the instigation of a friend, Hardie St. Martin. He showed me a rough version he had done of a fever dream that occurs in the first part of the novel—ten strange pages, grave and vivid, very funny at moments, and full of abrupt shifts of tone and leaps of imagination (in these ways, not unlike some of Vallejo's poetry)—and the hook was sunk. Already a passionate admirer of the poetry, I was curious to see what his fiction would be like, and the long, grey Catalan afternoons lent themselves easily to the pleasures of writing prose and improving my eccentric, self-taught Spanish. My enthusiasm faded somewhat as I read through the book: the fever dream was a set piece, its language more poetic than anything that followed and its relation to the narrative not fully developed, and the final chapter was something of a disappointment—I began to feel that I had been reading a Marxist tract disguised as a novel. Still, much of the story was compelling, written as it was with headlong power and a sense of exigent haste, and I worked away at it until I had about forty pages that looked readable and passed the St. Martin inspec-

tion. When it was time to return to America, I put the work
aside in the press of other duties and more or less forgot about
it.

St. Martin periodically reminded me, his letters inno-
cently asking whatever happened to the Vallejo translation,
sighing that *someone* should do it. I knew he was right. Whatever its defects as art, however coldly one had come to regard
its politics, *El Tungsteno* was an influential book that, for more
than one reason, needed to be available in English.

César Vallejo is widely acknowledged as one of the great
poets of the century and one of the most important poets in
the Spanish language. Yet, although the poetry has been translated many times by many hands—looking up, I can see on
my bookshelves eight separate volumes of English versions—
the prose has been ignored, at least in the United States. In
1972, when I first read *El Tungsteno*, there was, as far as I
know, nothing of his fiction available in English. (Clayton
Eshleman says that some of it has not yet been published even
in Spanish.) This is a serious lack. We still read Whitman's
dreadful novel *Franklin Evans* and Yeats's *John Sherman*, princi-
pally because they are the work of important poets. But *El
Tungsteno* and, I might add, Vallejo's stories demand attention
not only because their author is a great poet, but also because
he had an impressive talent for prose fiction and, as you will
see, wrote many pages of riveting power and vivid beauty.

El Tungsteno is a species of agitprop, and it suffers from
most of the characteristic limitations of that genre. The moral
is urgent and insistent and always on the surface; the plot is so
constructed as to arouse rage and incite to action; with one
exception, its characters tend toward the stereotypical and pre-

dictable. But in spite of what I see as severe faults, *El Tungsteno* is not a tedious or mechanical book. Vallejo is writing about things he saw and experienced: he was himself half Indian, he worked in a mining town, he did some time in a Peruvian jail, he saw with his own eyes how peasants and workers were treated, and he became a devout and active communist. The vividness of his memory, his eye for detail, give drama and immediacy to the events of his story. And however melodramatic and broadly drawn his rendering, he did not have to invent them. The terrible conditions he observed were the conditions that Indians and mestizos endured, and to a large extent still do.

Although Vallejo does not permit himself the moral and political complexity that makes his poems so resonant and mysterious, he is enough of a storyteller to survive the programmatic dogma that dictates so much of his action. It is hard to turn away from the anger and suffering that breathe through these pages. The monopoly of power and wealth by the whites, the misery of the dispossessed, the destruction of Indian cultures—these are hard facts, like tungsten, that hard, dense, most heat-resistant of metals, so well suited to military vehicles and ordnance and so profitable to those who control its production. And others will be struck, as I have been, by the implacable connection Vallejo develops between the coldness and rapacity of the men toward both the land and its Indian inhabitants and their brutal and exploitative relationships with women. In spite of preachment and exaggeration, he has made a passionate document of a representative moment in modern Peruvian history and of the malign impact of certain North American corporations on the people of Peru, particularly the Indians of the sierra, a document that can help us to understand the hatred and fear that so many Third World intellectuals feel toward our country.

It is plain to see, and unforgivable not to acknowledge, in these late years of the century, how much human suffering has come from the practical application of Marxist doctrines — even more, I would guess, than from capitalist imperialism (though I leave such measurements to the scholars of comparative suffering) — and almost all will sneer or laugh at the party line so clearly laid down in this novel. But it is well to remember that it was written in 1931 (the same year that Vallejo officially joined the Spanish Communist Party), and its author did not have the advantage of our all-too-knowing hindsight. He made three brief visits to the Soviet Union and wrote a book about it, but it is highly unlikely he was given any chance to witness the real horrors of the regime, such as the collectivization of the Ukraine; he got to interview Mayakovsky. He spent most of the 1930s in Spain or traveling back and forth between France and Spain, raising money, writing, doing whatever he could to preserve the Spanish republic against the Fascist revolution, but he does not seem to have been aware of the cruel and cynical role played by the Communist Party in that tragic drama; he lacked the shrewd, worldly intelligence, the experience, and perhaps the vantage ground that enabled Orwell and Koestler to see with icy clarity what was going on. By 1938 Vallejo was dead, before the Hitler-Stalin pact, and well before the purge trials, the official murders, and the Gulag became matters of general knowledge in the West.

As Christopher Leland has said, *El Tungsteno* "belongs to that era of heady Marxist idealism ultimately destroyed by both rightist reaction and the gradual recognition of Stalinist brutality." And he adds, "There is something deeply moving in the effort of a world-class poet to produce a text as 'politically correct' as *El Tungsteno*." I too find it moving, and I am moved as well by the life, its exile and poverty and selfless labor. Vallejo's communism issued from the depths of his soul, inextricably entwined there with his Catholicism, his self-abnegation, his sense of sin. To me, it is worlds apart from Neruda's brand of Marxism with its vague, windy rhetoric, its Rotarian optimism, its big meals and fancy houses. Vallejo seems to have been tormented constantly by his consciousness of human cruelty. One might imagine that Servando Huanca, the hero of *El Tungsteno*, were he alive today, would be one of the exalted assassins of the Sendero Luminoso; I would like to believe that his creator would no longer find him quite so simple and sympathetic a hero.

I must address myself briefly to the most vexing problem this translation presented me with and how I have dealt with it. Although others more qualified to judge may disagree, my impression is that the prose of *El Tungsteno* is sometimes hasty and careless, and now and then a word is plainly illogical. (I have given an example or two in the notes.) It is not my business to "improve" the work of a great writer, but Vallejo was much too overworked in the last few years of his short life to do the careful editing and revision that the novel required. It is possible that some errors were introduced by the original publisher in Madrid; there are certainly many misprints in the later Lima edition that I worked from. Although I have taken pains to make my version as accurate as possible, I have considered that my first duty, both to Vallejo and to my own language, was to produce the clearest, most vigorous, most readable *Tungsten* that my American English is capable of. In performing it, I have silently emended a word here, a phrase there, and once or twice taken the liberty of dropping a few redundant words or a sentence. I sought the help and advice of several scholars, but then made my own decisions, for which I am fully responsible.

I owe a debt of gratitude to the Guggenheim Foundation, which made it possible for me to finish this work, and I cannot help thinking how strange it is to live in a world in which a great fortune made from Central and South American mines should then be devoted to fostering humane studies, some of which are bound to cast a harsh light on the making of such fortunes.

I also owe heartfelt thanks to Professor José Miguel Oviedo of UCLA and to my colleagues here at Pomona College, Howard Young, Michael McGaha, Ralph Bolton, Richard Barnes, and Thomas Pinney. I am also indebted to Professor Kevin O'Connor for several kindnesses and for supplying an introduction far beyond my capacities. My greatest thanks go to Hardie St. Martin, for acts of friendship too numerous to name and for a lifetime's devotion to Spanish, American, and Spanish American literature, a contribution to our culture too little known and too meagerly rewarded.

Robert Mezey

Claremont, California
Spring 1988

Tungsten

PART 1

Having finally gained control of the tungsten mines of Quivilca, in the state of Cuzco, the New York management of a North American corporation called the Mining Society ordered extraction of the mineral to begin immediately.

A horde of day laborers and clerks poured out of Colca and the roadside towns, heading for the mines. This flood was followed by another and another, all signed up for settlement and excavation of the mines. Not finding a sufficient work force in the immediate vicinity of the deposits, or anywhere within a radius of ten miles, the company was obliged to bring in from far-off villages and from the countryside a vast swarm of Indians, destined for work in the mines.

Money began to circulate faster and in quantities never before seen in Colca, capital of the province in which the mines lay. Business dealings grew to unheard of proportions. Everywhere, in wineshops and markets, streets and plazas, you could see people buying and selling, making deals. An enormous number of urban and rural estates changed hands, and the notaries public and magistrate courts simmered with endless coming and going. The dollars of the Mining Society had thrown the once placid provincial life into a commotion it had no experience of.

Everyone affected an air of being on the move. Even the manner of walking, normally slow and languid, became rapid and impatient. Men passed, dressed in khaki, in leggings and riding breeches, speaking (in voices that had also changed tone) of dollars, documents, checks, treasury seals, memoranda, cancellations, machinery, tons. Young girls from the outskirts came out to see them go by and trembled with a pleasant nervousness, thinking of the distant lode, which pulled at them irresistibly with its exotic charm. They smiled and blushed, asking,

"Are you going to Quivilca?"

"Sure. Tomorrow, very early."

"Aren't you something! Off to make your fortune in the mines!"

And so began the idylls and love affairs, which later would have to find shelter in the shadowy vaults of the fabled mine.

With the first wave of laborers and miners went the directors and high officials of the company. There were, to begin with, Mr. Taik and Mr. Weiss, the manager and assistant manager of the Mining Society; the treasurer, Javier Machuca; the Peruvian engineer, Baldomero Rubio; the merchant José Marino, who claimed exclusive rights as storekeeper and labor contractor for the Society; the commissioner for the mining district, Baldazari; and the surveyor Leónidas Benites, who was Rubio's assistant. Rubio brought his wife and two little boys. Marino had with him only his ten-year-old nephew, whom he was always beating. The others went without families.

Where they established themselves was a sparsely inhabited slope on the eastern flank of the Andes, which looked out over a region of forests. There they found—the only sign of human life—a small hut belonging to the Soras, the natives of the place. They would be able to use the Indians as guides in that bleak and unexplored region and this stroke of luck, coupled with the fact that the slope was topographically an ideal spot for company headquarters, led the mine personnel to throw up their tents all around the Sora hut.

Risky and strenuous efforts were made to dig in and set up a normal, well-organized life on those desolate plateaus and to begin work in the mines. Lack of communication with civilized towns, to which the place was barely linked by a rugged llama trail, proved in the first days an almost insuperable difficulty. Several times the work was stopped for lack of tools or because of the hunger and illness of the men, who had been subjected suddenly to the shock of a glacial and implacable climate.

The Soras, in whom the miners found every kind of support and a frank and cheerful gentleness, played a role that came to take on such tremendous importance that more than once, had it not been for their timely succor, the whole enterprise would have ended in total failure. When the provisions ran out and no more had come from Colca, the Soras gave of their grain, their cattle, their tools and energies, without stint or caution, and what's more, without any recompense. They were content to live in harmony and disinterested friendship with the miners, watching them with a certain childlike curiosity as they roused themselves night and day in a systematic struggle with fantastic and mysterious machines. For its own part, the Mining Society had no need, at first, of the Soras' labor in the work of the mines, since it had brought from Colca and the wayside towns a numerous and adequate work force. In this respect, the Mining Society left the Soras in peace, until the day when the mines might demand more men, more energy. Would that day come? For the time being, the Soras went on living apart from the activity of the mines.

"Why are you always doing that?" asked a Sora of a worker whose job it was to oil the cranes.

"It's for lifting out the waste."

"And why do you lift out the waste?"

"To clean the seam and free the metal."

"And what are you going to do with the metal?"

"Don't you like having money? What a stupid Indian you are!"

The Sora saw the workman smile and he smiled too, mechanically, without understanding. He went on watching him all day and for many days after, trying to see what this job of oiling cranes might lead to. And some time later, the Sora again questioned the worker, whose brow was streaming with sweat.

"You have money now? What's money?"

The worker answered in a fatherly way, making his shirt pockets jingle.

"This is money. Look here. This is money—do you hear it?"

The worker then took out several nickel coins to show him. The Sora stared at them like a creature who doesn't quite understand.

"And what do you do with money?"

"You buy what you want. What an idiot you are, boy."

The worker laughed again. The Sora went off, hopping and whistling.

Another time, another of the Soras, who was gazing fixedly, as if entranced, at a workman hammering on the anvil of a forge, started laughing with a clear and playful delight. The blacksmith said to him,

"What are you laughing at, sonny? You want to work with me?"

"Yes. I want to do that."

"No, hombre, you don't know how. This is very tough."

But the Sora kept on about working in the forge. In the end, they gave in and he worked there four days running, getting to the point where he was a real help to the mechanics. On the fifth day, around noon, the Sora abruptly put aside the ingots and took off.

"Hey," they called to him, "why are you leaving? Go on with your work."

"No," said the Sora, "I don't like it any more."

"They're going to pay you. They're going to pay you for your work. Just go on working."

"No. I don't want to any more."

In a few days, they saw the same Sora pouring water from a gourd into a tub in which a girl was washing wheat. Then he offered to carry one end of a rope in the shafts. Later, when they began hauling the ore from the pithead to the assayer's office, this same Sora was seen lugging the handbarrows. The merchant Marino, the labor contractor, said to him one day,

"Well, I see that you're working too. Okay, boy, you want an advance? How much do you want?"

The Sora did not understand this language of "advance" and "how much do you want." He wanted only to be active, to

work and amuse himself, and nothing more. For the Soras
could not keep still. They came, they went, cheerful, breathing hard, their muscles tensed and the veins standing out with
exertion, tending flocks, sowing, making mounds for seed-
lings, hunting wild vicuña and alpaca, or clambering up boulders or cliffs, in an incessant and, one might say, disinterested
toil. They had absolutely no sense of utility. Without calcula-
tion or worry about what might be the economic result of their
acts, they seemed to live life as an expansive and generous
game. They displayed so much trust in others that sometimes
they aroused pity. They knew nothing of how buying and selling worked, and from this ignorance arose some amusing
scenes.

"Sell me a llama for jerky."

The animal was delivered, without payment for what it
was worth, without even a request for payment. Sometimes
they were given a coin or two for the llama, which they took
only to pass it on to the first comer and at the slightest hint.

The mine personnel, the clerks and laborers, had scarcely
established themselves in the district when they turned their
attention to the necessity of augmenting the supplies carried
in from the distant town with whatever goods the place itself
could provide, such as beasts of burden, llamas for meat, edi-
ble grains and so forth. The trouble was that someone had to
carry out the patient work of exploration and clearing brush in
those wild tracts, to transform them into arable and fertile
land.

The first to set to work on the land, with a view not only to obtaining products for his own use but also to enriching himself through stock-raising and farming, was the store-owner and sole labor contractor of Quivilca, José Marino. In effect, he formed a secret partnership with the engineer Rubio and the surveyor Benites. Marino took on as his prerogative the management of this partnership, since from behind his counter he could take care of business with particular advantage and ease. Indeed, Marino had an extraordinary head for business. Short and fat, of a crafty and avaricious character, the merchant knew how to embroil people in his affairs, as the fox embroils the chickens. Baldomero Rubio, on the other hand, was a meek sort, in spite of his height and a slight curvature of the shoulders that gave him an astonishing resemblance to a condor waiting in ambush for a lamb. As for Leónidas Benites, he had not changed from the easily frightened student at the Lima School of Engineering, weak and squeamish, qualities worse than useless in business affairs.

From the beginning, José Marino had had his eye on the fields of the Soras, land already sown, and he resolved to gain possession of them. Although he had to compete for them against Machuca, Baldazari, and the others, who were also beginning to strip the Soras of their holdings, the merchant Marino came out the winner in this contest. Two weapons served him well in such matters: the store, and his absolute cynicism.

The Soras were seduced by what they saw in the store, rare things to their innocent and primitive minds: dyed flannels, picturesque bottles, multicolored boxes, matches, caramels, shiny buckets, transparent glasses and so on. The Soras felt drawn to the store like certain insects to the light, and José Marino did the rest with his loanshark's guile.

"Sell me the little plot next to your hut," he said to one of them one day in the store, taking advantage of the fascination in which the Soras stood speechless before the things on the shelves.

"What did you say, taita?"

"That you should give me your goose farm and I'll give you whatever you want from my store."

"All right, taita."

The sale, or rather, the exchange, was made. In return for the goose farm, José Marino gave the Indian a small blue carafe with red flowers.

"Careful you don't break it," said Marino solicitously.

Then he showed the Sora how he must carry the carafe, with how steady a hand, so as not to break it. The Indian, flanked by his two companions, slowly carried the little vase to his hut, step by step, like a sacred trust. They covered the distance—about one kilometer—in two and a half hours. People came out to have a look and nearly died laughing.

The Sora had not really given any thought to whether the business of trading his goose farm for a carafe was fair. All he knew was that Marino wanted his land and he gave it to him. The second part of the transaction—getting the carafe— the Sora perceived as separate and independent from the first part. The Sora had taken a fancy to the thing and he believed that Marino had handed it over to him solely because he had taken a fancy to it.

And in this very way the merchant went on annexing the seeded fields of the Soras, which they in their turn went on giving up in exchange for the pretty little trinkets in the store and in the greatest imaginable innocence, like children who do not know what they are doing.

The Soras, while on one hand stripping themselves of their possessions and cattle to the advantage of Marino, Machuca, Baldazari and the other high officials of the Mining Society, did not on the other hand cease from struggling with the immense virgin wilderness, contending with it in table-lands and lowlands, in thickets and on escarpments, finding fertile places to plough and fresh animals to subdue and breed. The despoiling of their interests did not seem to inspire in them the slightest sense of grievance. On the contrary, it was for them an opportunity to expend more energy, since their innate restlessness thus found its happiest and most efficient expression. The economic consciousness of the Soras was very simple: as long as they could work and had both the means and a place to work, to obtain what they fairly needed for living, the rest did not matter to them. Only on that day when the how and where of survival were lacking, only then would they really open their eyes and oppose their exploiters with a full-blooded resistance. Their struggle with the mine people would then be a matter of life or death. Would that day come? For the moment, the Soras lived in a kind of permanent retreat before the cunning and implacable encroachments of Marino and company.

The peons, for their part, condemned this swindling of the Soras with pity and compassion.

"What gall!" the workers would exclaim, crossing themselves. "To take away their land and even their houses. And drive them away from what belongs to them. What a bunch of thieves!"

"But it's really their own fault," one of the workers observed. "They're simpletons. If they get a good price, okay, and if they don't, that's okay too. If you ask them for their farm, they laugh like it was some kind of joke and give it to you on the spot. Just animals! Dumb animals! And they couldn't be more contented with their lot . . . ah, fuck 'em!"

The laborers saw the Soras as more or less crazy, out of contact with reality. One old lady, the mother of a collier, grabbed one of the Soras by his jacket, growling angrily,

"Listen, you fool! Why do you give your things away? Didn't you work for them? And now you're going to laugh? Don't you see? Now you're going to laugh . . ."

The woman flushed with exasperation and nearly pulled his ears off. The Sora, in response, went to fetch her an armful of new potatoes, which the old woman refused.

"Look, I'm not telling you this so that you'll give me something. Keep your damn potatoes!"

Then she was seized with an inexplicable regret, so that in the end she accepted the gift, turning on the Sora a gaze brimming with sympathy and tenderness.

Another time, a stonecutter's woman shed tears on finding the Indians so generous and defenseless, so utterly without guile or forethought. She had bought from them a crop of pumpkins, just picked, but, instead of giving them the promised amount, at the last moment she pressed some coins into a Sora's hand and said,

"Take four *reales*. It's all I have. Okay?"

"All right, mama," said the Sora.

But, as the woman needed to buy some medicine for her husband, whose hand had been shredded by a dynamite blast

at the seam face, and saw that she could still withhold from
the four *reales* a little something for that, she spoke to him
again, pleading,

"Better yet, take only three. I need the other."

"All right, mama."

The poor woman perceived that she could get away with
still another coin. She opened the Sora's hand and took out
one *real* more, saying with a timorous quaver,

"No, take two. I'll give you the rest another time."

"All right, mama," he answered again, impassive.

It was then that the woman lowered her eyes, melted by
the Sora's gesture of innocent goodness. She pressed into his
hand the two *reales* she would have used for her husband's
medicine, feeling herself shaken by an unfamiliar and profound
emotion which made her cry all afternoon.

Usually, after working hours, they all gathered in José Marino's store, to chat and drink brandy, all of them dressed in
heavy clothing and bundled in skins against the cold—Mr.
Taik and Mr. Weiss, the engineer Rubio, the treasurer Machuca, Commissioner Baldazari, and the teacher Zavala, who
had just arrived to take charge of the school. Sometimes
Leónidas Benites showed up too, but he drank almost nothing
and would leave very early. They threw dice there as well, and
if it was Sunday, there were pistol shots, heavy drinking, and
general swinishness.

At the beginning of the evening, they talked about the
news from Colca and Lima, then about the war in Europe.

Later they went on to topics concerning the exportation of tungsten, shares of which were rising daily on the stock exchange. Finally they got on to stories from the mines, slanderous local gossip about people's private affairs. When the subject of the Soras came up, Leónidas Benites said, with a philosophical air, in his creeping-Jesus voice,

"Those poor Soras! They're such cowards, such half-wits. They act like that because they don't have the guts to look out for themselves and they don't know how to say no. A weak and slavish race—it's unbelievable how submissive they are. They give me a pain, they really infuriate me."

Marino, already in his cups, took up the argument:

"No, don't you believe it. Don't you believe it. The Indians know very well what they're doing. What's more, that's life—conflict, an endless struggle between men. The law of selection. Someone's got to lose so somebody else can win. You, my friend, you less than anyone . . ."

These last words were spoken with pronounced sarcasm, out of that compulsion for outwitting and silencing others which was a dominant trait in Marino's character. Benites took his meaning and was visibly upset, at a loss to reply to a man who was not only a bully but very drunk. The rest of the group caught on, sneering and crying out as with one voice,

"Right! Of course! Absolutely!"

The engineer Rubio, scratching with a fingernail on the zinc counter, as was his habit, argued in a distant and stammering voice,

"No, sir. In my opinion, these Indians like their strenuous life, working, clearing virgin land, chasing wild animals. That's their custom, that's the way they live. They give all these things away only to throw themselves once more into rounding up new herds and putting up new shanties. And so they live happy and contented. They know nothing of property rights and think that anyone can take anything, indiscriminately. Remember that business of the door?"

"The door to the office?" asked the cashier, coughing.

"Exactly. That Sora just up and threw the door on his shoulder and carried it off to add to his corral, with the same nonchalance and assurance he'd have in picking up something he owned."

A loud burst of laughter resounded throughout the store.

"And what did they do with him? This is amusing."

"When they asked him where he was taking the door, he said 'To my cabin,' smiling with that funny childish innocence. Naturally they took it away from him. He figured that anyone who needed the door could just walk off with it. They're really funny."

Marino, winking and puffing out his belly, said,

"They just *act* stupid. They're good for nothing."

To this notion Benites took exception, with a grimace of pity and distaste.

"By no means, sir. They are weak. It's out of sheer weakness that they let themselves be robbed of what belongs to them."

Rubio was irritated:

"You call them weak, these men who face forests and mesas, in the midst of wild animals and every kind of danger, to eke out a living? How come *you* don't do that, nor any of us here?"

"That's not courage, my friend. Courage is fighting man to

man—the one who comes out on top, he's the brave one. All that other stuff is a very different thing."

"So, you believe that a man's strength, his courage, has been created for the purpose of getting the better of another man? Beautiful! *I* think that an individual's courage should be used for work, for adding to the collective wealth, not as a weapon against others. Your theory is astonishing!"

"Exactly. I am a person incapable of hurting anyone. Everybody knows that. But I believe I'm obliged to defend my life and my interests if anyone tries to take them away from me."

Marino chimed in,

"I'm not saying anything. Flies don't land in a closed mouth . . . What are you going to have? Who's ordering? Come on, enough of this babbling!"

The surveyor took no notice.

"For example, I've come here to work, not to let anyone take what I've made, but to save up the money I need. Aside from this, I take nothing from anyone, nor do I want to ride roughshod over any of the natives."

Marino grew tired of asking who was ordering drinks, and since Benites, his partner in the farming and livestock venture, was paying him no mind, absorbed as he was in the argument, the merchant said, with a laugh of biting irony, to make him shut up,

"I say nothing. Benites! Benites! Benites . . . remember, flies don't land in a closed mouth."

The treasurer Machuca, after a fit of coughing, tried to speak, the phlegm in his throat congested by his exertion:

"I'd say that . . ."

More coughing.

"What I mean to say is . . ."

He could not go on. He coughed for some time, and finally he was able to get it off his chest:

"The Soras are hard-hearted Indians, indifferent to someone else's pain, and they don't have much sense. Just the other day I saw one of them hanging by a cord, which a boy held fast at the other end, looped around his waist. The way the Sora worked and tightened the rope with the weight of his body, it looked like it was going to cut the other one in half. The boy had no way to get loose and he was kicking his feet from the pain, with his face turning purple and his tongue bulging out. The Sora saw it all and still he stayed on the rope, laughing like an idiot. They're unfeeling and cruel. Cold-hearted. They ought to be Christians and practice the virtues of the Church."

"Bravo! Well said! You ordering drinks?" asked Marino.

"Leave me alone, I'm talking . . ."

"First order . . ."

"Goddammit! Nothing else!"

Leónidas Benites was merely expressing in words what he practiced in the reality of his daily conduct. Benites was economy personified and he watched out for the least little cent with edifying zeal. Better days would come, when he would have piled up a bit of capital and could leave Quivilca, to set up his own business somewhere else. For now, he had to work and save, with nothing in view but the future. Benites was not unaware that in this world he who has money is happiest, and that, therefore, the great virtues are work and thrift, which procure a tranquil and righteous existence, without attacks on the property of others, without despicable intrigues born of greed and spite and other base inclinations, which end in the corruption and ruin of individuals and societies. Leónidas Benites liked to say to Julio Zavala, the schoolmaster,

"You should teach the children two things only: work and thrift. You could sum up all Christian doctrine in these two supreme maxims, which in my opinion are a synthesis of the morality of all times. Without work and without thrift, you can have neither clear conscience, charity, nor justice—nothing. That is the experience of history. The rest is rubbish!"

Then, growing agitated and imparting a tone of sincerity to his words, he added,

"A woman raised me and I live in gratitude to her for having given me what education I have. That's why I can carry on in the manner you all know, working day and night, struggling to create the right economic situation for myself, modest to be sure, but independent and honest."

And his chronic mask of anguish softened. His eyes shone. As if he were recollecting something, he explained to Zavala,

"Thrift is one thing, avarice is another. Between Marino and me, for instance, that's the difference between avarice and thrift. I know you follow me, my dear friend . . ."

The teacher made a sign that he understood, and appeared to ponder deeply the ideas of Benites.

The surveyor had, in general, a powerful and heartfelt conviction that he was a fine young man, industrious, well-ordered, destined for a bright and honorable future. He was always referring to his own person, setting himself up as a model of life which everyone should imitate. This was not explicitly stated but flowed rather from his very words, articulated with exemplary and apostolic dignity on those occasions when problems of morality and fate came up among his friends. At such times he speechified at considerable length on good and evil, truth and falsehood, sincerity and hypocrisy, and other lofty themes.

Due to the orderly life Leónidas Benites led, his health never failed him.

"But the day you do fall ill," bawled José Marino, who had set himself up in Quivilca as a quack doctor, "you'll never get up again."

Leónidas Benites, in the face of these somber words, took even better care of himself. The cleanliness of his room and his personal hygiene were wonderfully thorough in every detail, omitting nothing that anyone could fault. He was always looking out for his physical well-being, going through a series of actions which only he, patient and meticulous as a paranoid old man, could perform. In the morning, before leaving for work, he went through his various underclothes, to see which were most suitable for the prevailing weather and the state of his health; nor was it unusual for him to return home after getting halfway to work, in order to change his shorts or undershirt because it was colder than he thought or because the ones he had put on warmed him all too well. It was the same with his stockings, shoes, hat, pullover, and even with his gloves and his briefcase. If snow fell, he not only loaded up with the greatest possible number of papers, rulers, and plumblines, but also, for the exercise, got out his levels, tri-

pods, and theodolites, even though he had no use for them at
the time. Sometimes he could be seen shaking and leaping
and running like a madman, until he could hardly move. Other
times he would not leave his room for anything, and if someone came, he would open the door slowly and warily, lest a
snowdrift should suddenly force its way in. But if there was
sun, he threw all the doors and windows wide open and would
not willingly close them. So it happened that one day, Benites
being in the treasurer's office, the boy whom he had left guard-
ing the open door of his room wandered off, and someone got
in and stole the little stove as well as some sugar.

But this was not all. He was even more compulsive in
taking preventive measures against contagious diseases. From
no one would he accept so much as a morsel or a swig without
exorcising it in advance and making the sign of the cross over
it five times, neither more nor less. One Sunday morning
when the cook had kindly brought him a plate of hot cornbread, the treasurer came to see him and entered at the very
moment that Leónidas was making the third cross over the
cornbread. He lost count of the crosses and for that reason he
did not dare even taste the gift but gave it to the dog. He had
little stomach for extending his hand to another; when he saw
that he had no other choice, he would shake hands with a
gingerly touch of his finger tips, and then he would worry, a
look of disgust on his face, until he could go wash with two
kinds of disinfectant soap, which he never ran out of. Everything in his room was always in its place, and he too was
always in his place, working, meditating, sleeping, eating, or
reading *Self Help*, by Smiles, which he considered the finest
modern work. On religious holidays, he would leaf through

The Gospel according to St. Matthew, a little book tooled with gold, which his mother had taught him to love and cherish for all that it means to true Christians.

With the passage of time, his voice had weakened considerably, due to the snows of the cordillera. This condition seemed a defect of the worst sort in the eyes of José Marino, his associate, with whom he had frequent arguments on this score.

"Don't put me on!" Marino would say to him, in his sly tone, in front of all the habitués of the store. "Speak up like a man! Cut out all this meekness and sanctimoniousness. You're too old to play the fool. Drink well, eat well, find yourself a girl, and then you'll see how your voice clears up . . ."

Leónidas Benites answered something which could not be heard over the laughter provoked by Marino's stinging phrases. His partner shouted at him mockingly,

"What? How's that? What are you saying? What's the matter? Hell, he doesn't hear anything!"

The laughter redoubled. Leónidas Benites, wounded to the core by the jeering and sneering of the others, turned even redder and finally left.

In general, Leónidas Benites was not very well liked in Quivilca. Why not? Was it because of the kind of life he led, his passion for moralizing, his physical weakness? His isolation from the others and his distrust of them? The only person who remained close to the surveyor and looked on him with affection was a woman, the mother of a lathe worker, half deaf and already getting on in years, who had a reputation for piety and a high regard for good habits and the austere and exemplary life. Nowhere was Leónidas Benites at ease but at the cottage of this devout lady, with whom he had long conversations while playing cards, commenting on the life of Quivilca and, very often, sermonizing on the solemn themes of morality.

One afternoon they came to tell the señora that Benites was sick in bed. She went immediately to see him, finding him in fact besieged by a high fever that made him rave and mumble to himself in his misery. She prepared him an infusion of eucalyptus, very strong, with two cups of alcohol, and got ready everything she would need to give him a mustard plaster. In that way a copious sweat would be produced, a sure sign that the illness, which seemed to be nothing but a bad cold, had receded. But even after the two treatments and even after the sick man began to sweat, the fever persisted and even seemed to rise by the minute.

Night had fallen and it started to snow. The door and window of Benites' room were tightly sealed. The señora stuffed rags into the cracks, to prevent the slightest draft. A sperm-oil candle burned, laying sad yellow strokes on the edges of things and on Benites' bed. Depending on how he shifted or changed his posture in the restlessness of fever, the shadows flickered, now short, now long, broken off or clashing on the planes of his beetle-browed face and among the pillows and sheets.

Benites shivered and uttered the unintelligible sounds of nightmare. The señora, dismayed by the growing seriousness of her patient's condition, began to pray, kneeling before a picture of the Heart of Jesus which hung at the head of the bed. She bent her pale and impassive head, like a plaster death mask, and began to moan and beseech. At last she rose up revived. Standing next to the bed, she said,

"Benites?"

His breathing came quieter now and more even. The señora approached on tiptoes, leaned over the bed, and watched for a long while. Having reflected a moment, she called again, pretending to be calm,

"Benites?"

The sick man loosed a whimper of utter helplessness which struck her in every motherly fiber of her being.

"Benites? How do you feel? Shall I try something else?"

Benites made a brusque heavy movement, waved both hands in the air as if brushing away invisible insects, and opened his eyes, which were red and seemed almost filled with blood. His glance was vague and yet threatening. Making a cracking sound with his dry, purplish lips, he mumbled senselessly,

"Nothing! That curve is too big! Leave me alone! I know what I'm doing. Leave me alone!"

And he turned abruptly to the wall, drawing up his knees and burrowing into the bedclothes.

There was no doctor in Quivilca. The mine had sought one, but to no avail. Everyone dealt with his own illnesses as best he knew how, except when it came to pneumonia, in the treatment of which the quack Marino claimed to specialize. The good lady who was nursing Benites did not know whether to call in the merchant, in case it were pneumonia, or take it upon herself to get hold of some other medicine without further delay. In her agitation she walked back and forth through the room, back and forth. Every now and then, she looked closely at the sick man or pressed her ear against the door, listening to the fall of the snow. It was possible that her son might come looking for her or that someone else might pass by whom she could ask for advice or assistance.

At times, the sick man was sunk in an absolute silence, which the señora in her deafness did not notice, but for the most part the night wore on filled with painful cries and delirious babble. All there was nearby, by way of a neighbor, was a vast deposit of tungsten. Everything else lay at some distance off, high up on the slope of the hill, and one had to shout to be heard.

The señora decided to prepare another remedy. Among the useful things which Benites kept as a precaution on his little table, she found a bit of glycerin, which suddenly suggested to her a new medicine. She relit the little stove. Then tiptoeing close to the bed, she had a long look at the patient, who had been quiet for a little while, and she perceived that he was asleep. She made up her mind to let him rest, putting the treatment off till later, in case the fever continued. She knelt down beneath the holy picture and for some while, in a vehemence of grief, she muttered long prayers punctuated by sighs and sobs. At length she arose and came again to the sickbed, drying her tears on the hem of her muslin blouse. Benites went on sleeping peacefully.

"God is very great!" avowed the señora, deeply moved, her voice barely audible. "Ay, divine Heart of Jesus!" she added, lifting her eyes to the icon and clasping her hands, flooded with ineffable rapture. "You can do everything! Watch over your creature. Take care of him, don't abandon him. By your sacred wounds! O Father, protect us in this vale of tears!"

She could not contain her emotion and began to weep. She took a few steps and sat down on a bench. There she remained, almost falling asleep.

Suddenly she came awake. The candle was about to gutter out. It had melted in a curious way, making a deep, wide arch through which the molten sperm oil was moving, gradually piling up on one edge of the candlestick and cooling into the shape of a closed fist with the index finger pointed toward the flame. She saw to the candle and, noticing that Benites was still sleeping and had not changed position, she bent over to look at his face. "Sleeping," she said, and again decided not to wake him.

During his fever dreams, Leónidas Benites had looked up many times at the picture of the Sacred Heart of Jesus that hung at the head of his bed. The divine image mingled with the images of his delirium, framed in the reddish aura of the whitewashed wall. His hallucinations had to do with the things that worried him most in the real world, things like his duties at the mines, his business partnership with Marino and Rubio, his ambition to save enough money to go to Lima to finish his engineering studies as soon as possible and get started on a business of his own in that field. In his delirium he saw the merchant Marino making off with his money and threatening to pummel him, backed up by all the settlers of Quivilca. Benites protested fiercely but had to beat a hasty retreat before so large a mob of assailants. He stumbled as he fled over steep, rocky ground and, making an abrupt turn round a bend in the rugged terrain, he blundered into another bunch of his enemies, which made him jump for fright. The Heart of Jesus immediately joined the fray and scared off all the thugs and thieves with His mere presence, only to vanish suddenly, leaving Benites alone and defenseless at the exact moment that an infuriated Mr. Taik was saying to him,

"Get out of here! The Mining Society is cancelling your appointment, on account of the lousy job you've done. Out of here, you sneak!"

Benites pleaded with him, wringing his hands piteously. Mr. Taik ordered two of his flunkies to throw him out of the office. Two Soras came over grinning, as if to mock him in his humiliation. Seizing him by the arms, they dragged him away and gave him a savage push. Then the Heart of Jesus came to the rescue with such dispatch that everything was all right again. Then the Lord vanished in a flash of lightning.

Right after that, Benites caught a Sora stealing a bundle of bills from his strongbox. He threw himself on the culprit, belaboring him, enraged not so much by the amount he was taking as by the cynical, jeering laughter of the Indian, who was suddenly mounted on the back of an alligator in the middle of a great river. Benites went right down to the water's edge and was just about to enter the current when he felt himself suddenly growing torpid and immobile. Now gilded by a radiant halo, Jesus appeared to Benites again. All at once the river spread until it covered every inch of space as far as the eye could see. A vast multitude surrounded the Lord, alert to His slightest intention, and an intense mood of decision filled the horizon. Benites was seized by sudden terror, realizing dimly but beyond a doubt that he was present at the hour of the Last Judgment.

Benites then set about examining his conscience so that he might make out his place in eternity. He tried to recall all the good and evil he had done on earth. First, he recalled the good things he had done. He collected them greedily and put them in a prime spot, visible to his mind's eye and arranged in strict order of importance: at the bottom, those acts that arose from a more or less insignificant or debatable goodness, and higher up, within easy reach and yet above all the others, those that came of great strokes of virtue, whose merit announced itself far and wide, leaving no doubt of their authenticity and transcendence. Then he searched his mind for bitter memories, and his mind had none to give him. Not one single gnawing memory. From time to time, a faded image crept timidly in, but examined carefully, in the light of reason, it ended by disappearing into those neutral slots in the hierarchy of values, or weighed even more delicately, came to lose every tinge of guilt, to be replaced not by some vague color but by its very opposite: such a memory turned out to be, at bottom, that of some worthy act, which Benites then acknowledged with a satisfaction that could only be called paternal. Fortunately, Benites was intelligent and had taken pains to cultivate his reflective and critical powers, which he could now use to probe deeply into things and assign them their true and precise meanings.

The dreaming Benites had an intimation that he would be facing his Saviour before very long. As he considered it, an overpowering terror drove him deeper and deeper into his own thoughts. He was distracted by the memory of an alfalfa farmer from Accoya whom he hadn't seen in years, from whom his mother used to buy greens for her guinea pigs, with many a curse for his miserliness and avarice. By a rapid association of ideas, Benites recalled that sometimes he himself had loved money, perhaps inordinately. He recalled that in Colca

one night, in a huge cheerless room where he was sleeping
alone, he had heard the noise of souls in torment. In the
darkness, they started pushing against the door. Benites was
frightened and made no sound. He remembered that when
next day he told some neighbors what had happened, they all
assured him that the spirits were often in torment in that
house because buried treasure had been left there by a Spanish colonial agent. With the nightly repetition of these noises,
Benites was finally aroused by a lust for gold. And one midnight, when they came to push against that door flooded in
shadow, the surveyor addressed the tormented souls.

"Who is it?" he asked, sitting up in bed, his teeth chatter-
ing with fear.

There was no answer. The pushing continued. Anxiously,
in a cold sweat, Benites asked again,

"Who's there? If you are a soul in torment, tell me what
you want."

A nasal voice, that seemed to come from the other world,
answered in a piteous, mournful tone:

"I am a soul in torment."

Benites knew it was a sin to run from suffering and urged
it in the next breath,

"What's wrong? Why are you in torment?"

The voice was on the verge of tears.

"I left five cents buried in a corner of the kitchen. Because
of them I can't be saved. Throw in another ninety-five cents
and pay the priest for a mass for my salvation . . ."

Irritated by the unexpected and troublesome turn the
affair was taking, Benites growled, lashing out at the soul in
torment,

"I've seen some shameless dead people in my time, but this takes the cake!"

On the following day, Benites checked out of the inn.

Going over all this in his dream, now that he was a long way from his life on earth, he found his behavior sinful and deserving of punishment. And yet, after long thought, he decided that his insulting words to the tormented soul had been dictated by an abnormal state of mind and carried no evil intent. He was not forgetting that, from a moral point of view, actions have the appearance given them by the intention behind them and by that intention alone. As for not paying for the mass requested by the spirit, it had not been *his* fault but rather the parish priest's, whom a severe dyspepsia was keeping away from the church at the time. Let it be said in passing that it did not escape Benites that said priest's illness was not serious enough to excuse him altogether from discharging sacred duties. Finally, after a more judicious and sober analysis, he reflected that perhaps it hadn't really been a soul in torment after all, but just a big practical joke by one of his friends who knew he was losing sleep over the rumored treasure. This being the case, it was lucky there had been no mass, for the prank would thus have turned into a mockery and a sacrilege, with Benites caught in the middle as one of its prime movers. Well, no doubt about it, he had done well, acting as he had, subconsciously standing up for serious statutes of the Church, and consequently his conduct would furnish sufficient merit for a reward from his Savior. Moved by such singular and unshakable logic, Benites set this virtuous act in the very center of all his memories.

A feeling he had never before been sensible of, a feeling

that issued from the very depth of his being, suddenly told him that he was in the presence of Jesus. At this moment his mind was flooded with so much light that he was possessed by the whole perfect vision of what was, is, and will be, total awareness of time and space, the rich, full, and unified image of all things, the eternal and essential sense of boundaries. A flash of wisdom enveloped him giving him, an understanding at once emotional and sensory, abstract and physical, darkling and bright, odd and even, fragmented and whole, of his permanent role in the divine destiny. And at that moment he could do nothing, think, want, or feel nothing, exclusively for himself or within himself. His personality, like the I of the egoist, could not distinguish itself from the friendly and collaborative shape of his own haunches. A rich chord of the infinite had lodged itself in his being, as the passage of Jesus and His heavenly banner brushed the powerful antenna of his heart. After a little, he came back to himself, and feeling himself cut off from God, like a fractured number, broken loose from the harmony of the universe, condemned to drift at random through a grey and featureless immensity, without dawn or sundown, his soul was filled to overflowing with an indescribable pain he had never felt before; it was drowning him, as if he were chewing some bitter wool of darkness, unable even to swallow. The cause of this deep agony, this black misery of his spirit, was not the loss of Paradise but rather the expression of infinite sadness he saw, or sensed he saw, shadowing the divine face of the Nazarene. Ah, as he knelt before Him, what mortal sadness was the Lord's, that not even the double-spouted urn of the Enigma could hold it! For that terrible sorrow Benites suffered hopeless and boundless grief.

"Lord," he whispered, entreating, "at least don't let Your sorrow be so great! At least let a little of it come into *my* heart! At least let the little stones come and help me to reflect Your great sadness!"

Silence reigned in that transcendent space.

"Lord! extinguish the lamp of Your sadness, for I haven't the heart to reflect it! What have I done with my blood? Where is my blood? Dear Lord! You gave it to me and look how I left it clotted in the depths of my life, unwittingly, miserly with it, poor with it. Lord! I was the sinner, I was Your poor stray sheep! When it was in my power to be timeless Adam, without noon, without evening, without night, without the second day! And when I could have checked and silenced for all eternity the muttering in Eden and saved the Absolute in the midst of Change! When I could have realized my limits smoothly and easily, as in simple bodies, claw to claw, beak to beak, pebble to pebble, apple to apple! When I could have torn apart the paths, lengthwise and crosswise, down the middle from top to bottom, to see if that way I could go out to meet the Truth! Lord! I was the miscreant, I was Your ungrateful and unforgivable worm! When I could even not have been born! When at least I could have made myself eternal in the cocoon and in the evening before birth! Happy are the cocoons, for they are the native jewels of paradise, though horny stamens sleep in their sealed bellies! Happy the nights before, for they have not fallen and will never fall in actual time! I could have been merely egg, nebula, latent and immanent rhythm—oh, God . . ."

This cry of infinite desolation burst from Benites and, fading away, left the silence voiceless forever.

Benites awakened abruptly. Morning light flooded his room. Next to his bed stood José Marino.

"What a soft life, partner!" cried Marino, his arms folded. "Eleven o'clock and still in bed! Come on, get up! I'm going to Colca this afternoon."

Benites was taken aback.

"To Colca? Today you're going to Colca?"

Marino impatiently walked the length of the room.

"Yes, sir! Now get up. We're going to settle some accounts. Rubio's already waiting for us in the store."

Sitting up in bed, Benites shivered.

"Okay. I'm getting up right now. I still have a bit of fever but it doesn't matter."

"Fever, you? Don't play games, hombre. Just get up—get up. I'll wait for you in the store."

Marino went out and Benites began to get dressed, taking his usual precautions: stockings, undershorts, undershirt, shirt, all had to be perfectly matched to whatever gauntlet his health might have to run. Neither too much clothing nor too little.

At one in the afternoon, the horse José Marino was to ride was standing saddled at the door of the shop. Marino's nephew held him by a rope. Inside the store, they were arguing in loud voices, with explosions of laughter. The accounts having been settled, Marino's two partners, Rubio and Benites, the treasurer Machuca, the schoolmaster Zavala, Commissioner Baldazari, Mr. Taik and Mr. Weiss were there to say goodbye to the merchant. There were many toasts. Machuca, already a little drunk, was needling Marino:

"And who're you leaving La Rosada with?"

Graciela—La Rosada—was one of Marino's girlfriends. A

young woman of eighteen, a classic highland beauty with great dark eyes and bright innocent cheeks, she had been brought from Colca by a timekeeper at the mine as his mistress. Drawn by the mystique of the mining life, which pulled at the ignorant and deluded villagers with a strange and irresistible force, her sisters, Teresa and Albina, followed her. The three runaway girls ended up in Quivilca. Their parents, wretched old peasants, mourned for them for a long time. In Quivilca, the girls set about working, making and selling chicha, and so they were often obliged to drink and get tipsy with their customers. The timekeeper soon got fed up with Graciela and the kind of work she did, and left her. After a few weeks, José Marino took her on. As for Albina and Teresa, many rumors flew about in Quivilca.

Marino responded flippantly to Machuca's repeated questions.

"We'll throw the dice for her, if you like."

"That's the ticket! Throw the dice! But let's all play for her," shouted Baldazari.

A circle formed around the counter. All of them, even Benites himself, were drunk. Marino rattled the dice-cup loudly, crying,

"Who goes first?"

He threw the dice and counted, pointing with his fingers at each of the men in turn:

"One, two, three, four—your play!"

It was Leónidas Benites on whom it fell to make the first cast.

"But what are we playing for?" asked Benites, dice-cup in hand.

"Just roll 'em," said Baldazari. "Didn't you hear us say

we're playing for La Rosada?"

Benites was upset in spite of his drunkenness:

"No, hombre! To throw dice for a woman! That's not right! Let's play for a drink!"

Reproaches, insults, raillery from everyone drowned out Benites' timid scruples, and the game began.

"Bravo! Let him pay for a round! We'll celebrate each roll with a drink."

Commissioner Baldazari won the game for La Rosada and ordered champagne all around. Machuca sidled up to him, saying,

"That's some tasty dark meat you're gonna eat, Commissioner! You got yourself a nice piece of ass." And the treasurer opened his arms in a circle and made a leering and obscene face. The Commissioner's eyes glittered too as he called La Rosada to mind. He asked Machuca,

"But where's she living now? I haven't seen her in a while."

"Over by La Poza. Hey! Send for her right now!"

"No, hombre, not now. It's broad daylight. People can see us."

"What do y' mean, people! All the Indians are at work. Send for her. Come on!"

"I said no. It's just a joke anyway. You think Marino is going to give up this broad? If he were leaving for good, sure, but he's just going to Colca for a few days."

"So what? What's won is won. Act like you have some balls! That's some intoxicating pussy. Me, I like the crudeness of it. Send for her! Besides, you're the commissioner and you give the orders. Don't be ridiculous—these other guys are just assholes. Go on, Commissioner!"

"You think she'll come?"

"Sure she'll come."

"Who is she living with?"

"Alone, with her sisters, and they're fantastic too."

Baldazari stood there considering, tapping his riding whip.

A few minutes later, José Marino and Baldazari went out the door.

"Take a walk, Cucho," said Marino to his nephew. "Go to the house of the Rosadas and tell Graciela to come here, to the store, that I'm waiting for her, because I'm leaving now. If she asks who's with me, don't tell her. Say that I'm alone, absolutely alone. Got it?"

"Yes, uncle."

"Make sure you don't forget. Tell her I'm here alone, there's nobody else in the store. Leave the horse. Tie it to the leg of the counter. Now go on! But fast! I want you back here right away!"

Cucho looped the horse's bridle rope around the counter leg and ran off to do his errand.

"Fly, fly!" Marino and Baldazari cried after him.

José Marino fawned on everyone who might be useful to him in one way or another, and his servility to the Commissioner knew no limits. Marino pandered to him even in his sexual adventures. They would go out at night with a gendarme to inspect the workers' encampments and the mine operations. Sometimes in the wee hours, Baldazari would stay behind in some poor hut or shanty to sleep with the wife, or sister, or mother, of a man on the night shift. The gendarme would go back alone to headquarters, and Marino, also alone, to his store. Why did the merchant serve and flatter the Commissioner? There were several reasons. For the time being, the merchant was going to be away and he had asked the Commissioner as a favor to keep an eye on transactions at the store, which the schoolmaster Zavala, now on vacation, was left in charge of. Then, too, the Commissioner was now spending lavishly in the bar and inducing others to do the same. It was 3:00 P.M. and already José Marino had sold many bottles of champagne, cinzano, brandy, and whiskey. But these were all merely momentary reasons, and rather trivial; there were others more serious and long-standing. Commissioner Baldazari was the labor contractor's right-hand man in the signing up of laborers and in his dealings with the directors of the Mining Society. When Marino was not getting anywhere with a worker, when the man refused to go along with Marino's figures, or to accept a particularly low wage, or to work the nightshift or on holidays, Marino enlisted the Commissioner's aid, and he would change the peon's mind with a night in jail or with a truncheon (the original punishment in Peruvian prisons) or with lashes. Likewise, when Marino could not directly obtain from Mr. Taik and Mr. Weiss this or that advantage, accommodation, or whatever favor or edge, Marino would wheel up Baldazari, who would intervene with the full power of his influence and authority and get the bosses to give Marino whatever he was after. It was therefore in no way surprising that the merchant now stood ready to hand over his woman to Baldazari, in public and just like that.

A little while later, Graciela appeared at the corner with Cucho. The men inside the store had hidden themselves. Only José Marino could be seen at the door, trying to conceal his drunkenness.

"Come on in," he said sweetly. "I'm leaving soon. Come on. I've sent for you because I'm going away."

Graciela said timidly,

"I thought you were just going to leave, without even saying goodbye."

A sudden guffaw burst from the store and everybody came out at once to confront Graciela. Blushing, dumbfounded, she stumbled against the wall. They surrounded her, some reaching out to touch her, others chucking her under the chin. Marino, breaking up with laughter, said,

"Sit down, sit down. This is our farewell. What'll you drink? Our friends! Our bosses! Our dearly beloved Commissioner! Sit down! What'll you have?"

They closed the door halfway, and from outside Cucho pulled loose the horse's rope and sat down in the doorway to wait.

Snow fell. From time to time people came to buy things at the store and left without daring to go inside. An Indian woman, grief-stricken and frantic, came hurrying up.

"Is your uncle here?" she asked Cucho, panting.

"Yeah, he's here—why?"

"He has to sell me some laudanum. I'm in a terrible rush—my mama is dying."

"Go on in, if you want."

"But maybe he's got people in there."

"He's with a lot of guys. But go on in, if you want."

The woman hesitated and stood waiting at the door. A growing anguish suffused her features. Cucho, still holding on to the rope, amused himself by drawing the national coat of arms with a red pencil stub on a scrap of his school notebook.

The woman paced up and down, desperate yet not daring to enter the store. She caught a glimpse of what was going on inside, listened awhile, and then paced some more. She asked Cucho,

"Who's in there?"

"The Commissioner."

"Who else?"

"The treasurer, the engineer, the schoolmaster, the two gringos . . . they're all good and drunk. They're drinking champagne."

"But I hear a woman!"

"Graciela."

"La Rosada?"

"Yeah. My uncle sent for her since he's leaving."

"Oh, my God! When are they going? What time?"

The woman began to moan.

"Why are you crying?" Cucho asked.

"My mama is dying and Don José has people with him!"

"If you like, I'll call my uncle and he'll wait on you."

"But maybe it'll make him angry."

Cucho peeped inside and called tentatively,

"Uncle Pepe!"

The orgy was at its height. From the store came an unintelligible babble, mixed with laughter and shrieks and a sickening odor. Cucho called several times. At last José Marino came out.

"What do y' want, you little shit?" he snapped at the boy.

Cucho, seeing him drunk and in a rage, jumped back, intimidated. The woman too moved to one side.

"For you to sell some laudanum," Cucho mumbled, keeping his distance.

"Laudanum my ass, you little sonofabitch!" Marino roared, throwing himself furiously at his nephew. He slapped him very hard across the face and knocked him down.

"For Christ's sake!" shouted the merchant, kicking the boy with his booted toe. "You little shit! You're always fucking around with me!"

Some passersby drew near to defend Cucho. The woman who wanted the laudanum begged Marino on her knees,

"Don't hit him, taita! He only did it for me, because I asked him. Hit me if you want, hit me!"

He kicked the woman. Blind with rage and alcohol, he went on lashing out wildly for several seconds, until the Commissioner came out and restrained him.

"What's all this, my dear Marino?" he said, holding him tightly by the lapels.

"Forgive me, Commissioner," Marino answered meekly. "A thousand pardons!"

The two of them went into the store. Cucho lay in the snow, crying and smeared with blood. The Indian woman stood over him, sobbing miserably.

"Just for calling him, he hits him. Just for that! And me too, just because I wanted a little medicine!"

A muscular young Indian appeared, weeping and running hard.

"Chana! Chana! Mama just died. Come! Come! She's just died . . ."

And Chana, she who had come for the laudanum, began to run, following the young man and weeping.

José Marino's horse, spooked, had run off. Cucho, drying his tears and blood, went to look for him. He knew all too well that for the horse's running away, "it would be his ass," as his uncle used to say when he threatened to whip him. Luckily he came back with the animal, and sat down once more at the door of the store, which remained half open. Crouching, he peered furtively in. What was going on in there now?

José Marino, drink in hand, was behind the door, in private conversation with Mr. Taik, manager of the Mining Society. He was speaking to him in a flattering and ingratiating tone:

"But, Mr. Taik—I've seen it myself, with my own eyes . . ."

"That's very kind of you, but it's risky business," replied the manager, grinning and very red in the face. They were speaking of Rubio's wife.

"Yes, yes, of course. But all you have to do is give the word. Mr. Taik, I know what I'm talking about. Rubio's a sick man. She doesn't love him. In fact, she's dying for you, I've seen her."

The manager was smiling fixedly.

"But, Señor Marino, Rubio might find out."

"I assure you, Mr. Taik, he won't know anything about it. I stake my life on it."

Marino finished off his drink and added firmly,

"Would you like me to take Rubio with me one of these days, out of Quivilca, so you can do what you want?"

"All right, we'll see. We'll see. Thanks a lot. You're very kind."

"Where you're concerned, Mr. Taik, you know that I don't hold back in anything. I am your friend—a very unassuming one, to be sure, very meek and very humble, the last in line, who knows, but a true friend and ready to serve you even with

my life. Your humble servant, Mr. Taik. Your humble friend!"
Marino bowed grandly.

At that moment, Mr. Weiss called out to the merchant
from the other end of the store,

"Señor Marino! Another round of champagne!"

José Marino flew to fill the glasses.

Meanwhile, Graciela was already very drunk. José Marino,
her lover, had given her a strange concoction which he had
prepared secretly. One glass of this liquor had quite intoxi-
cated her. The Commissioner said to Marino, aside and in a
low voice,

"Incredible! Incredible! You're really something. She's already in another world."

"And that," answered Marino boastfully, "that without laying too much of the green stuff on her. Otherwise, her tongue
would have been hanging out long before now."

He hugged Baldazari, adding,

"You deserve it all, Commissioner. For you, everything.
Not just a mickey! Not just a woman! For you, my life! Believe
me."

During the spasms brought on by the doctored drink,
Graciela sang and cried mindlessly. Suddenly she would break
off and dance by herself. Everyone clapped out the rhythm,
amid laughter and lewd endearments. Holding a glass in one
hand, reeling, her shawl falling off, Graciela said,

"I'm just a poor unlucky girl. Don José! Come over here!
What am I, compared to you? Please, I'm just a poor girl,
that's all . . ."

There was still more laughter and shouting. Then José
Marino, hanging on to the Commissioner's arm, said to Gra-

ciela, as if she were blind, and for everyone to hear,

"You see? This here is the Honorable Commissioner, the law, the most important person in Quivilca, not counting our bosses, Mr. Taik and Mr. Weiss. D'you see him, right here with us?"

Her eyes glazed with drink, Graciela tried to make out the Commissioner.

"Uh huh, I see him. Yeh . . . hon'able 'missioner . . . uh huh . . ."

"Fine. The Commissioner will take care of you while I'm away. You understand? He'll look after you. He'll take my place in everything, for everything . . ."

As he said this, Marino leered, mocking her, and added,

"Do everything he tells you to, just like it was me. You hear me? You hear me, Graciela?"

Graciela answered, her words slurred, her eyes almost closed, "Yeh . . . aw right . . . aw right . . ."

Then she staggered and nearly fell. Machuca, the treasurer, let out a horselaugh. José Marino gestured at him to shut up and winked at Baldazari, to let him know that the honeypot was ready. The others, in a chorus of low voices, were all urging Baldazari on:

"Now, Commissioner! Get into her, just stick it in!"

The Commissioner only laughed and went on drinking.

Clutching at the counter to keep from falling down, Graciela started to sit, yelling,

"Don José! Come over here next to me! Come . . ."

José Marino once more hinted to Baldazari that it was time to approach La Rosada. Baldazari's only answer was to have another drink. In a few minutes he was blind drunk. He went on downing the champagne. The others were equally smashed, completely out of their minds. Rubio was shouting at Mr. Taik about international politics while Zavala, Leónidas Benites and Mr. Weiss were in a huddle with their arms around one another. José Marino and Commissioner Baldazari were circling Graciela. At one point, La Rosada threw her arms around Marino, but he slipped smoothly aside and put Baldazari instead in Graciela's arms. The girl caught on and peevishly pushed the Commissioner away.

"Kiss the Commissioner!" Marino ordered her angrily.

"No!" cried Graciela with fresh energy, as if she were coming to.

"Leave her alone," Baldazari told Marino.

But the labor contractor was already in a fury and he insisted:

"I told you to kiss the Commissioner, Graciela!"

"No! I won't, not ever! Not ever, Don José!"

"You won't kiss him? You won't do what I tell you? Just you wait!" the merchant snarled, and went to mix another mickey.

As night came on, they closed the door tight and the store sank into darkness. And then, all those at the party—except Benites, who had fallen asleep—acquainted themselves, one after another, with Graciela's body. First José Marino and then Baldazari had generously offered the girl to their friends. The first to tear into this warm flesh were, of course, the bosses, Mr. Taik and Mr. Weiss. The other characters then got into the act, in the order of their social and economic rank: Commissioner Baldazari, the treasurer Machuca, the engineer Rubio, and the schoolmaster Zavala. Out of modesty, gallantry, or delicacy, José Marino went last. He accompanied himself with a demonic commotion. He spewed forth into the darkness cries and exclamations absolutely hair-raising in their filth and depravity. And throughout this harrowing performance he kept up an obscene chatter with his accomplices. A choked, muffled snore was the only sign of life from Graciela. José Marino finished with a hideous phlegmy laugh . . .

And when the lights were turned on in the store, there were broken bottles and glasses on the counter, champagne spilled all over the floor, torn clothing thrown here and there, and haggard, sweaty faces. Here and there a bloodstain darkened on the cuff or collar of a shirt. Marino fetched a basin of water for them to wash their hands. As they stood in a circle washing, a pistol shot rang out, sending the basin flying toward the ceiling. A guffaw twisted the mouth of the Commissioner, for it was he who had fired.

"That was to test my men!" Baldazari said, pocketing his revolver. "But I see that everyone is shook up."

Leónidas Benites woke up.

"Where's Graciela?" he asked, rubbing his eyes. "Is she already gone?"

Wiping his glasses, Mr. Taik said:

"Señor Baldazari, we ought to wake her up. Seems to me it's time she went back to her cabin. It's late."

"Sure, sure," the Commissioner said, looking serious. "We have to wake her up. Go ahead, Marino, you're always our man."

"Ah," the merchant exclaimed, "that won't be so easy. There's no cure for a mickey except sleeping it off."

"Well, anyhow," Rubio argued, "she can't be left lying like that on the floor. Don't you agree, Mr. Taik?"

"Oh, by all means," said the manager, puffing at his pipe.

Leónidas Benites went over to Graciela, the others trailing behind him. La Rosada lay sprawled on the floor, motionless, disheveled, her skirt askew and still hiked halfway up her thighs. They shouted her name, shaking her hard, but she showed no sign of waking up. They brought over a candle. They called and shook her again. Nothing. She remained motionless. José Marino laid his ear on the girl's breast and the others waited in silence.

"Shit!" the merchant spat, getting up. "She's dead!"

"Dead?" they all cried, stupefied. "Don't talk nonsense! It's impossible!"

"Yes," Graciela's lover said, quite unruffled. "She's dead. Some fun we had."

Then Mr. Taik said in a low, hard voice,

"Okay. Don't anybody go shooting their mouth off. You hear me? Not one word. She must be taken home now. Her sisters must be told that she's had a fit and they have to let her get some rest. And tomorrow, when they find her dead, everything will be okay."

The others agreed, and that was how it was done.

At ten that night, José Marino mounted his horse and rode off to Colca. On the following day, Graciela was buried. In the front row of the funeral procession walked the Commissioner of Quivilca, along with Zavala, Rubio, Machuca, and Benites. Cucho, the nephew of the dead girl's lover, followed at a distance.

All the men who had been in the store came back from the graveyard talking among themselves, cool and unconcerned, all except Leónidas Benites, who was deep in thought. The surveyor was the only one of that whole crowd in whom Graciela's death had left a certain heaviness and even a kind of remorse. In his heart, Benites knew that La Rosada had not died of natural causes. True, he had seen nothing of what happened to Graciela in the darkness, since he had been in a deep sleep the whole time, but he suspected the truth, if only in a shadowy and tentative way. On returning from the burial, Benites locked himself in his room, feeling guilty about the events of the previous night, a feeling he wasn't used to and which at first revolted him, and he stretched out on his bed to ponder it. Soon he fell asleep.

During the afternoon of that same day, Teresa and Albina, the two sisters of the dead woman, showed up in Mr. Taik's office at the Mining Society's headquarters. They were in tears. Two other Indian women, chicheras like the Rosadas, accompanied them. Albina and Teresa asked to speak with the boss and after a short wait, they were brought before the yanqui, who was at the time closeted with his countryman Mr. Weiss, the assistant manager. Both of them were sucking at their pipes.

"What can I do for you?" Mr. Taik asked drily.

"We've come here, master," said Teresa tearfully, "because everyone in Quivilca is saying that Graciela didn't just die, she was murdered. They say that it's because they got her drunk at the store, because of that. And that you, good master, should see that justice is done. How can they kill a poor woman that way and nothing happens to any of them . . ."

She could not go on for her tears.

Mr. Taik, extremely irritated, shot back,

"But who says these things?"

"Everybody, sir, everybody . . ."

"Have you lodged a complaint with the Commissioner?"

"Yes, master. But he says it's nothing more than gossip and not true."

"So? If that was the Commissioner's answer, why do you come here? And why are you still paying attention to nonsense and idiotic tales? Forget all that foolishness and go back home quietly. Death is death and the rest is just craziness and pointless whining . . . Go on! Off with you!" Mr. Taik added paternally, preparing to go out himself.

"Go on!" repeated Mr. Weiss, also in a defensive tone, sucking on his pipe and walking past them. "Don't pay so much attention to foolish talk. Go on, go home. Let's not have any impertinence or any more song and dance. Please . . ."

The two bosses, full of dignity and absolute authority, showed the Rosadas to the door, but Teresa and Albina, not weeping now, cried out angrily,

"It's only because you're the bosses! That's why you can do whatever you want, throw us out this way, and only for coming to complain! You're the ones who killed our Graciela! You killed her! You killed her!"

A servant came and, shoving them roughly, threw them out. The two girls went off sobbing and protesting, followed by the other chicheras, they too sobbing and protesting.

PART 2

José Marino went to Colca on urgent business. There he had another store, which was usually managed by his younger brother, Mateo. The Marino brothers also had in Colca an "employment agency" to lure peons to work in the Quivilca mines. In short, the firm of Marino Bros. consisted on one hand of the stores in Colca and Quivilca, and on the other of the recruitment of workers for the Mining Society.

The Mining Society had signed a contract with Marino Bros., the chief stipulations of which were as follows: Marino Bros. would have exclusive rights in supplying the yanqui corporation with as large a workforce as was necessary for the exploitation of the Quivilca deposits, and secondly, exclusive rights in the provision and sale of staples and other merchandise to the mining population of Quivilca, as a means of facilitating the hiring and rehiring of labor. Marino Bros. were thus set up as middlemen—on one hand, the real bosses of the workers, and on the other, agents or instruments of the North American corporation.

This contract with the Mining Society was enriching the Marino brothers with incredible speed. From the simple small

47

businessmen they had been in Colca before the discovery of tungsten in Quivilca, they had been transformed into great captains of finance whose name was beginning to be known all through central Peru. Just the movement of merchandise in their Colca and Quivilca stores represented substantial sums of money. At the time of José Marino's visit to Colca, just after the orgy and the death of Graciela in Quivilca, Marino Bros. were about to decide whether to buy up some gold deposits in a river basin in Huataca. This was the main reason for José Marino's trip.

But after supper, on the evening of the very day he arrived, the Marino brothers, in the course of a long discussion, had their attention abruptly and repeatedly drawn to various difficulties in the collaring of workers for Quivilca. Before leaving Quivilca, José Marino had had an extensive conversation with Mr. Taik about this matter. The New York office was demanding a speed-up in the extraction of tungsten in all their holdings in Peru and Bolivia. The mining syndicate pointed out the imminent entrance of the United States in the war in Europe and the consequent need for the corporation to stockpile as quickly as possible a great quantity of metal ready for transport, at a telegraphic order from New York, to the shipyards and munitions factories of the United States. Mr. Taik had put it flatly to José Marino:

"You get me a hundred more workers for the mines inside of a month."

"I'll do what I can, Mr. Taik," answered Marino.

"Oh no, don't give me that. You have to do it. For businessmen, nothing is impossible."

"But Mr. Taik, keep in mind that it's very hard just now to get workers from Colca. The Indians no longer want to come. They say it's too far. They want better wages. They want to bring their families along. The enthusiasm of those first days is long gone . . ."

Mr. Taik, sitting stiffly at his desk, sucked on his pipe and terminated Marino's excuses with implacable finality:

"Right, right. One hundred more workers within a month. Without fail."

And Mr. Taik solemnly rose and left the office. José Marino, subdued but still complaining, followed a few steps behind. But this sort of conversation, let it be said, far from cooling the friendship of the two men—if you could call it friendship—made it all the stronger. José Marino returned to the store and his first thought was to get Mr. Taik, through the mediation of his friend Machuca, to come to the merchant's farewell party.

"Bring Mr. Taik and Mr. Weiss."

"That's not going to be so easy."

"No, hombre, but bring them. Pretend it's your own idea and don't let on that I told you to. Tell them they don't have to be here for more than a few minutes."

"It can't be done. The gringos are working. You know they only come to the store in the afternoon."

"Listen, pal, just go. Go along, my dear treasurer, it's already close to lunchtime."

Machuca went and managed to persuade the two yanquis to come. At which José Marino practically dissolved in showering attentions and obeisances on Mr. Taik, none of which, of course, altered by one iota the directive of the Mining Society concerning the tungsten earmarked for the United States and the war.

"Before they left," José Marino was telling his brother, "I spoke to the gringo once more about this business, and once again he told me that it wasn't his doing, he just had to carry out the syndicate's orders, like it or not."

"But wait," argued Mateo, "what do we do now? We won't be able to find any Indians in Quivilca or on the outskirts. And the Soras?"

"The Soras!" echoed José, laughing at him. "It wasn't very long ago that we sent the Soras to the mines and it wasn't long after that that they disappeared. Stupid savage Indians! They all died in the shafts, out of stupidity, because they didn't know their way around the machinery."

"What now?" Mateo asked again, in anguish. "What's to be done? What can we do?"

"How many workers have we given advances to?" asked José in response.

Leafing through the receipt book, Mateo said,

"Twenty-three who should have left for Quivilca this month, before the twentieth."

"Have they been called? What do they say?"

"I've seen a few, nine of them, about two weeks ago, more or less, and they assured me that they'd leave for Quivilca at the end of last week. If they haven't gone, I'll have to see them again and get them to leave."

"Is the subprefect here?"

"Yes, of course he's here."

"Good. Then all we have to do is ask him for two troopers

first thing in the morning to go after those half-breeds right away. Where do they live? Look in the receipt book."

Mateo leafed again through the receipts, reading aloud, one by one, the names and addresses of the indentured workers. Then he said,

"Cruz, Pío, old man Grados, and the half-breed Laurencio— the soldiers can find them all together tomorrow. From Chocoda to Conra and then to Cunguy, all in one swoop . . ."

José stopped him abruptly.

"No, no, no. We have to see them all tomorrow, the nine you mentioned, at dawn or even while it's still dark."

"Okay, sure. Why not? We can do that. We'll give each of the soldiers a buck, a kick in the ass, a few coca leaves and cigarettes, and there you are . . ."

"Done!" cried José in conclusion.

The two of them moved restlessly about the room, shod in yellow boots, wearing great silk bandanas around their necks and "hot devil" outfits. The Marino brothers were originally from Mollendo. Some twelve years ago they had set out to make their way in the sierra, starting to work in Colca in a decrepit little stall on Commerce Street, where the two of them lived and sold various necessities: sugar, soap, matches, kerosene, salt, chili peppers, raw cane, rice, candles, pasta, tea, chocolate, and rum. Where did they get the cash to set up a business? Nobody knew for sure. All that was known was that in Mollendo they had worked as porters at the railroad station and that there they had put together four hundred *soles*, their total capital when they arrived in the highlands. How and when did they rise from working-class manners and morals to those of bourgeois merchants? Did they, once they became proprietors of a shop in Colca, continue, in their secret social hearts, to be the old workingmen of Mollendo? The Marino brothers leapt out of their social class one June night in 1909. The metamorphosis was pathetic. The historical leap was cruel, bloody, and almost geometrical, like certain circus acts.

It was the name day of the mayor of Colca, and the Marino brothers were invited, among others, to dine with the mayor. It was the first time that they found themselves asked to mingle with good society in Colca. The invitation came out of the blue, so unexpected that the Marinos, at first, laughed in an ecstacy at once half-animal and dramatic. For it so happened that neither one of them had the nerve to face so formidable an undertaking. In the anxious embarrassment of imagining themselves in the midst of aristocrats, neither José nor Mateo wanted to attend the banquet. Their proletarian lungs could not breathe such air, and because of this they quarreled. José told Mateo that he must go to the party, and Mateo said no, José must go. They decided it on the toss of a coin: heads or tails. Mateo lost. He put on his cashmere suit, his cloth hat, a shirt with celluloid collar and cuffs, a tie, and new patent leather shoes. Mateo felt rather elegant and was even beginning to regard himself as a true bourgeois, except that his shoes began to feel tight and cause him considerable pain. It was the first time he had worn them and he had no other pair worthy of such an occasion. So, sitting down and grimacing with pain, he said,

"I'm not going. It hurts too much. I can hardly walk."

José pleaded with him:

"But it's the mayor! Think of the honor of going to dine with his family and with the subprefect, with doctors, with the best people in Colca! Go! Don't be an idiot! If you go to this banquet, they'll invite us everywhere from now on, the judge, the doctor, even the deputy when he comes. And then we too will be thought of as respectable people. Everything depends on tonight. And you'll see. It's all a matter of getting in with the right circles and everything else will follow—success, money, respect. With good relations we'll have it all. How long are we going to remain laborers and no-accounts?"

It was already getting late, nearly time to be arriving at the banquet. After much entreaty from José, Mateo, rising above the pain of his shoes, heroically faced the ordeal of going to the party. His suffering was indescribable. He went limping, unable to escape. As he entered the mayor's house, before a crowd of curious townsfolk, he stubbed his foot against something or other and the stab of pain made him see stars. He was half leaping in torment at the very moment that the mayor's wife appeared at the door to welcome him, whereupon, without knowing how he did it, he transformed his agonized hopping into a courtly bow, improvised but irreproachable. Mateo greeted her with perfect decorum—

"Señora, a great honor! . . ."

Clasping her hand, he went in to take his seat, his step firm, easy, almost lithe. The historical bridge, the gulf between one class and another, had been safely crossed. As the mayor's wife said to her husband, some days later,

"Why, it turns out that Marino is a dear! We must invite him again."

The Marinos had no family in Colca except Cucho, Mateo's son by a chichera who had run off to the coast with another lover. Mateo lived now in a large house which was

attached to the store, both house and store the property of
Marino Bros. There, in one of the rooms of the house, the
two were now discussing their various transactions and
projects.

"And how do things stand in Quivilca?" asked Mateo after
a while.

"So-so. The gringos are impossible. Mr. Taik most of all,
he wouldn't give his grandmother a break. A hard case. He's
got me by the short hairs."

"But you have to know how to handle him, brother."

"Handle him?" repeated José with bitter sarcasm and dis-
belief. "You think I haven't already tried a thousand ways? The
gringos are a couple of assholes. Almost every day I get the
two of them to come to the store, through Machuca, or Rubio,
or Baldazari. They come, they drink. I invite them all the
time. I often fix them up with women. We go on sprees to the
laborers' camp. I've invited them to supper many times. I even
pimp for them."

"That's it. That's how you have to do it."

"You want to know what I put in Taik's head?" said José,
laughing. "I know that he's hopelessly cunt-struck, so I told
him that Rubio's old lady is dying for him. I told him the day I
left, since he had just been fucking me over on this business of
the workers. I thought I'd get in his good graces so that he'd
forget his demand for a hundred workers in one month, or at
least ease up a little."

"And how'd it turn out?"

"Nothing. The gringo just laughed like some moron.
Meanwhile, Rubio comes closer and closer to catching on.
Then I wanted to get him drunk, and he still wouldn't relent.

Finally I called Baldazari over and told him to find a way of getting to him, sort of underhanded, but that didn't work either. He just played dumb with Baldazari. Final score—zero."

"But tell me the truth, is Rubio's woman in love with him, or did you make it up?"

"What are you talking about, in love with him! I dreamed it up to flatter him, and to see what would happen. If the gringo had been hot to trot, Rubio's woman and Rubio himself would have pretended to see nothing. You know well enough what Rubio is—as long as he gets something out of it, he'll even sell his wife's ass."

"Okay," said Mateo. "We'd better get some sleep now. You're tired and we have a lot to do tomorrow. Laura!" he cried, stopping at the door.

"I'm coming, señor!" answered Laura from the kitchen. A buxom and rosy Indian girl, brought down from the highlands at the age of eight and sold by her father, a wretched share-cropper, to a curate in Colca, Laura had been passed along by the priest to an aged lady who owned a farm in Sonta, and then raped and carried off, two years ago, by Mateo Marino. Laura performed in the house of Marino Bros. the multiple role of cook, laundrymaid, housekeeper, handservant, and Mateo's concubine. Whenever José came from Quivilca for a few days, Laura generally shared his bed too, on the sly. Mateo had suspected it from the first and gradually passed from suspicion to certainty. But the Laura game did not seem to discompose the Marino brothers. On the contrary, the maid's arms seemed to bind them even more closely together. What in other men would have kindled jealousy, quickened brotherliness in the Marinos.

When Laura entered the room, the two men studied her at length out of the corners of their eyes, José with appetite and Mateo somewhat suspiciously. While Laura was serving dinner, the two brothers had taken no notice of her, absorbed as they were with their business affairs, but now that drowsiness was coming on and bedtime drew near, Laura suddenly awakened a lively attention in the Marino brothers.

"Is José's bed ready?" asked Mateo.

"All ready, señor," answered Laura.

"Good. Have you fed the horse?"

"Yes, señor. I threw him a bunch of alfalfa."

"Good. Now then, later when it gets colder, take off his saddle and throw him another."

"Very well, señor."

"And first thing in the morning, walk over to One-Eyed Lucas's and tell him to bring me the black mule. Tell him to be here no later than nine o'clock, without fail, because I have to go out to the farm."

"Very well, señor. Do you need anything else?"

"No. You can go to bed."

Laura made a submissive gesture of obedience.

"Good night, señores," she said and went out with her head bowed.

The Marino brothers stared brazenly at Laura's strong slender body as she timidly withdrew, at the garnet petticoats covering her down to her ankles, the high shoulders, the lithe and narrow waist, the straight black braided hair, the sensuous grace of her movements.

José and Mateo slept in the same room. Once they put out the candle and got into their beds, complete silence fell over the entire house. Neither of them were sleepy but both pretended to be asleep. Were they thinking about business? No, they were thinking about Laura, who was now making up her bed in the kitchen. Abruptly there was the sound of the girl's footsteps. Then, the faint rustle of the straw pallet being unrolled. Sitting down to patch a shoe, Laura sighed. And she, what was she thinking about? About going out to unsaddle the horse and throw him some more alfalfa? No, Laura was thinking about the Marino brothers.

Having been immersed since childhood in provincial life, she had acquired a little refinement, picking up many of the manners and conventions natural to a young lady of the village. She knew how to read and write. With the pittance Mateo paid her, she secretly bought herself earrings and scarves, white handkerchiefs, and cotton stockings. She also bought herself one day a copper finger-ring and high-heeled shoes. Every other Sunday she went to Mass, very early, before her master and lover woke up. But most of all Laura was filled with a vague and dreamy sensuality. She was twenty years old. Did she desire a man now and then? Never. But she would have loved to be in love. For her master she felt mostly hatred, albeit a concealed hatred, gilded or muffled by the vanity of being seen as the mistress of Señor Mateo Marino, one of the most notable personages in Colca. But the hatred was real. Privately Laura felt revulsion toward her master, a florid forty-year-old, rather bleary-eyed, puny, vulgar, filthy, as greedy as his brother, a man who, for his part, felt not the slightest affection for his kitchenmaid. When there were guests in the house of Marino Bros., Mateo made a great show of irritable and abusive contempt for Laura, so that no one might suspect what everyone knew: that he was her lover. And this wounded Laura deeply.

Her relationship with José was different. Since José could not take her openly and by force, inasmuch as she belonged to his brother, he won her over and held onto her by means of guile and deceit. He gave her to understand that Mateo was a fool, that he did not care for her and would do with her, sooner or later, what he had done with Cucho's mother: subject her to misery, forcing her to run off with the first man who came along. He told her that he, José, on the other hand, loved her deeply and would make her his household mistress the day that Mateo abandoned her. Moreover, José, unlike Mateo, who never promised Laura anything, constantly promised her money, although in fact he never gave her any. In short, José knew how to inveigle her, flattering her and pretending passion, something that Laura never found in Mateo. The very kind of guilty relations that bound them encouraged José on the one hand not to be cold and brutish like his brother, and on the other led Laura—a woman, when all was said and done—to prolong this game with the Marinos indefinitely. In this game there was also, on Laura's part, a good deal of vengefulness toward Mateo for his abuses. All things considered, neither did Laura care much for José Marino. She was not sure if at bottom she did not detest him as much as she detested his brother. But in any case, she felt that whatever there was between José and her, it was something very unstable, tenuous, pale, and spiritless. Often, when she thought about it, Laura realized that she felt nothing for this man. And if she thought longer, she came to admit to herself finally that she hated him . . .

Thus Laura mulled things over, mending her shoe.

The Marino brothers in their beds also mused, José long-ingly, on Laura, and Mateo with a certain uneasiness, on Laura and José. He wanted to go to the kitchen. He did not want José to go to the kitchen. José hoped that Mateo was sleeping. Even if he was convinced that Mateo knew every-thing, he was now equally sure that Mateo would pretend to notice nothing and that sooner or later he would go to sleep. Nevertheless, José's assumptions did not quite correspond with what Mateo really thought and wanted. Tonight, for the first time, Mateo felt a kind of vague and unfocused jealousy. The truth was that José's imminent trip to the kitchen caused Mateo pain. Why? Why such pangs tonight and not all the other nights?

A long while passed, things standing so in Laura's head and in the double head of Marino Bros. Then they heard Laura go out to unsaddle the horse and toss him another bit of alfalfa. The sound of her footsteps was soft, sensuous, almost velvety, and lust leapt up in José. He felt the need to swallow his saliva and could not keep from doing it. Mateo, hearing his brother swallow, was sure that he was awake, and the flame of jealousy leapt up in him.

Laura came back to the kitchen and abruptly closed the door. The Marino brothers trembled. What did it mean, that brusque closing of the door? José told himself that it was a tacit sign by which Laura meant to let him know that she was thinking about him and that the night was propitious for dalli-ance. Mateo was torn between this belief and the notion that Laura, by slamming the door, was trying to convey to him, Mateo, her resolute and irrevocable decision to remain faithful. But José could no longer contain himself. He turned violently in his bed. Then came the soft rustle of straw as the young girl lay down and stretched her body out on the pallet. At this moment lust overcame both men equally. Each felt as if he were lying on a bed of coals. The sheets were wildly tangled. The air was full of images . . . For a moment, and unbeknownst to either of them, José and Mateo were lying with their backs turned toward each other.

Mateo suddenly leapt out of bed, and José, hearing him, felt all the blood rush into his head. Where was Mateo going? José was flooded by a violent animal jealousy. Mateo softly pushed open the door and stepped barefooted out to the hallway. He knew that his brother could hear every sound, but when all was said and done, he was officially the master of this woman, and he was deranged with desire. José then heard Mateo scratching at the kitchen door, a scratching in which Laura recognized her nightly possessor. José's teeth chattered in fury as he stood with ear glued to the bedroom door. Would Laura open? She hesitated a moment, until Mateo himself wondered if she would let him in. But finally the habit of servitude triumphed over her. As Laura began slowly to slide out of her bed of straw, Mateo, standing tiptoe in the darkness and going out of his mind with his desire and Laura's slowness, scratched again at the door, this time loudly. In her haste Laura stumbled over the washtub and he heard her fall. At last the door opened and Mateo, trembling with lust, went in. José, having imagined the entire scene down to the tiniest detail, lay down again. The torment of his thirsty flesh and the growing realization of what was going on in those moments between Laura and his brother made him squirm in anguish among the sheets and squeezed from him the strangled howls of a poisoned animal.

What was happening in the kitchen was happening on the floor. Laura had fallen against the washtub and injured her wrist, shoulder, and hip. She moaned softly and her wrist bled. But nothing could restrain Mateo's lust. At first he took her hand, caressing it and licking away the blood. A moment later, he brutally shoved aside the wounded wrist and, as always when he finished, began to grunt like a gorged animal. Neither Laura nor Mateo had thus far said one word. Mateo got to his feet, and with great care made his way to the door, went out, and slowly closed it. He paused at the end of the hallway and pissed for a long time. José felt a hot rush of blood run through his limbs, and pulled the blankets over him, covering even his head. As Mateo entered the room, a hot and corrosive sweat ran down José's broad back.

Laura remained prostrate on the floor, weeping. She tried to get up but couldn't. Her hip hurt so much she thought it might be broken.

Once back in bed, Mateo felt cold. The way he figured it, he was certain that José, although he seemed to be sleeping, was not asleep. Would José insist on going to the kitchen? Very likely. José was always hot to go to the kitchen. But Mateo was no longer jealous of his brother. Thinking of José in Laura's arms did not trouble him. A heavy and irresistible torpor began to invade him, and when, a few minutes later, José opened the door in his turn and went out, Mateo, snoring deeply, did not hear him.

José violently pushed open the door to the kitchen and went in. Laura sat up quickly in spite of her pain. José groped for her in the darkness. At last he touched her. His avid sweaty hand, falling like a fat spider on the kitchenmaid's half-naked breast, made her catch her breath. A long and forcible kiss joined those lips still wet with tears to José's hard and greedy mouth. Laura stopped crying and her body yielded to him. Laura wanted José, now—but not José exactly. Any other man, so long as he was not Mateo, would have produced in her the same response. All that Laura needed to react that way was contact with anyone but her stupid and all too familiar daily master. And if this new embrace was passionate, yielding and, above all, cloaked in the shadow of the forbidden, it is even clearer why Laura received José Marino in a way she had not received Mateo Marino. Laura, a country girl as we have said, had acquired many characteristics of a young lady of the town, and among them, a taste for sin.

As José entwined himself in the kitchenmaid's arms, there arose from her body a pungent and disturbing odor. José sensed the strangeness of it and for a moment he did not move. What was that odor—half woman and half mystery—that engaged his nose, discomfiting him? Where did it come from? Was that how Laura smelled? Instantly José thought of his brother. A shudder of modesty went over him, a turbulent and all too human modesty. Yes, Mateo had just passed that way. His male blood sank, sliding like a runaway colt at the edge of a cliff. But this lasted only a moment. The fallen animal halted once more, and then, blind and heedless, went on his way.

If we keep in mind that José was merely toying with Laura and that his caresses and promises came to an end with the satisfaction of his lust, we will not be surprised that José withdrew from Laura a few minutes later, saying contemptuously in a low voice,

"And for this I waited hour after hour . . ."

"But listen, Don José," Laura pleaded, "don't leave. I want to tell you something . . ."

"What?" said José, annoyed and keeping his distance.

"I think I'm pregnant."

"Pregnant? Don't kid me!" said José with a derisive snort.

"Yes, Don José, it's so. I know I'm pregnant."

"And how do you know?"

"I throw up every morning."

"And since when do you think you're pregnant?"

"I don't know. But I'm almost positive."

"Ah," snarled José, in a temper, "just what I need! What does Mateo say?"

"I haven't told him anything."

"You haven't said anything to him! And why haven't you said anything to him?"

Laura was silent. José insisted,

"Answer me. Why haven't you told him?"

This *him* resounded and rose up between José and Laura like a dividing wall between two beds. Laura and José both knew quite well the meaning of the word. This *him* was the putative father, and José said *him* meaning Mateo, while for Laura, *he* was not necessarily Mateo, but José. And that was why the girl again answered nothing.

"Who needs this!" José said, getting ready to leave.

Laura tried to detain him with a moan.

"Yes, yes, because I'm not pregnant by your brother but by you."

José jeered in the darkness,

"By me? Pregnant by me? You want to drop my brother's

little bundle at my feet?"

"It's true, Don José, I'm pregnant by you. I know it! I know it! I know it!"

As her words were drowned in sobs, José countered, "But I haven't been with you for more than a month now."

"Yes, yes, yes! It was the last time. The last time . . ."

"But you can't know anything like that! How can you know, when more often than not you've slept with Mateo and me the same night?"

Laura at this moment felt distinctly uncomfortable. Was it the sweat? The position of her body? Her injuries? She changed position and felt something shift deep in her flesh. Immediately a dark, towering doubt loomed over Laura's heart. As a matter of fact, how *was* she to know which of the two Marinos was the father of her child? At that very moment she felt obscurely burdened, she felt the mingled blood of those two men vaguely beating in her womb. How to tell them apart?

"But how can you know?" José asked again, imperiously.

Laura was about to utter some absurdity but she held her tongue. No. It could not be the child of the two Marino brothers. A child never has but one father. The kitchenmaid, feeling herself at the limit of her terrible uncertainty, burst into deep, wrenching sobs. José went out and quietly closed the door.

The next day, at ten in the morning, the Marino brothers went to see Subprefect Luna about the matter of the peons.

When they arrived at his office, Luna had just finished shaving.

"Before we do anything," said the old subprefect in a hearty tone, "you're going to taste something choice."

From the other room he brought a bottle and some glasses, adding in his exhilaration,

"Try to guess where this comes from."

"From Chang the Chinaman?"

"No, sir," cried Luna, pouring the brandy himself.

"Old Monica?"

"Her neither."

"From the judge's house?"

"Hardly."

José took the first glass and tasted it.

"The priest Velarde?"

"You guessed it!"

"But it's fantastic!"

"Terrific!"

"Perfect! It's the cat's nuts!"

After his third glass, Mateo said,

"My dear Subprefect, we need a couple of gendarmes."

"What for, hombre?" old Luna replied in a joking mood, already a little drunk. "Who needs to be shot?"

José explained.

"We want to go see a few missing workers. What can a guy do? The Mining Society says we have to put a hundred peons in the mineshafts inside of a month. The New York office is calling for more tungsten. And the half-breeds we've given advances to are refusing to comply with their contracts and leave for Quivilca."

The subprefect, putting on a grave face, argued his case.

"But the fact is, I have no gendarmes at my disposal right now. The few that I have are not enough to pick up my conscripts. As you know, I'm on the spot too. The prefect insists that I produce at least five conscripts for him by the first of next month. And the half-breeds have turned into smoke! I don't have but two in the jail. That's all," he said, turning toward the door of his office which overlooked the plaza, and shouting loudly: "Anticona!"

"Your Excellency!" answered a gendarme, appearing immediately, coming to attention and giving a military salute from the door.

"Did the gendarmes go after the conscripts?"

"Yes, Excellency."

"At what time?"

"At one this morning, Excellency."

"How many went?"

"The sergeant and three soldiers, Excellency."

"And how many gendarmes are there in the barracks?"

"Two, Excellency."

"You see!" cried the subprefect, turning toward the Marino brothers. "I have barely enough for duty. No more than barely enough. It's a joke! And these same gendarmes are always goldbricking and malingering. They won't back me up. They're rummies. They're lazy. As long as they bring me conscripts, I promise to promote them and reward them, I give them their brandy, their coca, their cigarettes, even permission to do whatever they want to the Indians. Lash or sabre, I don't care. All I care about is that they bring me people, without stopping to think about it."

Luna's face took on an expression of chilling cruelty. The orderly, Anticona, saluted again and at a nod from the subprefect withdrew. The subprefect walked up and down, frowning in thought, and the Marino brothers stood there, very worried.

"When will the gendarmes come back with the conscripts?" José asked.

"This afternoon, I guess, about four or five."

"Good. Then they can go with us to get the peons tonight, say, between eight and nine."

"We'll see. Since they got up so early, they'll want to take it easy tonight."

"Now what?" cried José, very upset. "Look, the Mining Society is demanding . . ."

"Otherwise," Mateo broke in, "I mean if we don't get the gendarmes we need, we'll have no way of doing what the company wants."

For in Peru, and particularly in the sierra, the padrones use the police to force the workers to honor their civil contracts. The worker's obligation can be compelled by armed force, handled as if it were a crime. Worse yet, when a worker is "assisted," that is, given an advance, and thus sells his labor, binding himself to deliver it to the industrial enterprise, national or foreign, on a more or less specific date, and does not come through on the date stipulated, he is pursued by the authorities as a criminal. Once he is captured, no excuses will do; he is coerced into providing the promised services. It is, in short, a system of forced labor.

"Well," responded the subprefect in a conciliatory tone, "in the end we'll find a way to reconcile these concerns. We'll see. We have time . . ."

The Marino brothers, hearts sinking, muttered in unison,
"Very well, just as you say."

The subprefect fished out his watch.

"A quarter to eleven!" he exclaimed. "At eleven there's a
meeting of the Military Draft Commission."

And at that very instant the members of the Commission
began to arrive at the subprefect's office. The first to appear
was the mayor, Parga, an ancient bushwhacker from Cáceres,
very old and bent, sly, and a cold-blooded swindler. Then
came, together, the claims court judge, Dr. Ortega, the local
physician, Dr. Riaño, and the reigning celebrity of Colca,
Iglesias, the richest landlord in the province.

Dr. Ortega suffered from incurable boils. Originally from
Lima, he had been a magistrate in Colca some ten years. A
macabre story was told about him. He had had a girlfriend,
Domitila, whom, it seems, he came to love to the point of
mania. But a year ago Domitila had died. People said that Dr.
Ortega could not get her out of his mind, and that one night, a
few weeks after the funeral, the judge went secretly, and in
disguise, to the graveyard and exhumed the corpse. He was
accompanied in this business by two men he trusted completely. These two were involved in serious criminal proceed-
ings, and the judge had let them off in exchange for their
services that night. But why did Dr. Ortega perform such a
disinterment? It was said that once they had dug up the body,
the judge ordered the two men to leave him, and he was alone
with Domitila. It was said that the solitary act—seen by none
but spoken of by everyone—which Dr. Ortega committed on
the body of the dead woman was something unspeakable,
hair-raising. Did it really happen? Was it even believable? The
judge, from the moment of Domitila's death, took on a taci-

turn, enigmatic, and even queer and disturbing air. He seldom
went out. It was also said that he was now living with
Genoveva, a younger sister of Domitila. What psychic mael-
strom, what morbid disease, lay beneath the surface of this
man's life? Bearded, half lame, with scarf or bandage always at
his throat, shawled and remote, when he walked down the
street or attended an official function, he gazed vaguely across
his spectacles. Seeing him, people felt oddly and painfully ill
at ease. Some held their noses.

Dr. Riaño was new in Colca. A young man of about thirty,
from a respectable family in Ica, he dressed elegantly and had
an easy and florid way with words. He was given to declaring
himself an idealist and an ardent patriot, but he could not hide
what he really was, an extreme snob and social climber. A
bachelor and a good dancer, he had the local girls crazy about
him.

As for old Iglesias, the facts were simple: he was the sole
owner of four-fifths of the urban real estate in Colca. He also
boasted a fabulous ranch where he ran cattle and raised cash
crops. This ranch, Tobal, was so vast, its population of serfs so
numerous, and its herds so huge, that Iglesias himself did not
know exactly what he was worth. How had he acquired so
immense a fortune? By means of usury, and at the expense of
the poor. His depradations were so shameless that they came
to be the theme of folk songs and popular dances. One of
them went like this:

> Now I know who you are—
> you're the master of Tobal, you tread
> on the sweating necks of the poor,
> and you rob them of their bread—

on the sweating necks of the poor,
and you rob them of their bread—

A large family surrounded the old cacique. One of his sons, the eldest, was finishing his medical studies in Lima and had already announced his candidacy for the provincial assembly.

The subprefect Luna had had a long and stormy adminis-trative career. Retired captain of police, gambler and woman-izer, he displayed an extraordinary talent for political intrigue. Not once in the last ten years had he been out of public office. He got on very well with all the deputies, ministers, prefects, and senators. Nevertheless, because of his ferocity and impru-dence, he did not last long at any one post; he seemed to have run through almost the entire gamut of subprefect, commis-sioner, guard officer, military commander, and so on and so forth. A single thread unified his administrative career: the bloody incidents, riots, and insurrections that he provoked everywhere, the result of his entanglements, his excesses, and his depravity.

When the Marino brothers left the office, the meeting of the Draft Commission was declared open. The minutes were read by the subprefect's secretary, Boado, a lovesick young man with a face full of pimples, a hoarse voice, and excellent penmanship. Nobody had anything to add to the minutes. Then Luna said to his secretary,

"Make your announcements."

Boado opened various sealed documents and read in a loud voice:

"A telegram from the honorable prefect of the Department, which goes as follows: 'Subprefect. Colca. Request from you body quota end of month without fail. (Signed) Prefect Ledesma.' "

At that moment the plaza filled with the sound of mounted men along with the murmuring of a crowd. The subprefect abruptly interrupted his secretary:

"Hold it. Here come the conscripts."

The secretary looked out the door.

"Right. It's the conscripts," he said. "But there are a lot of people out there with them."

The Draft Commission adjourned the meeting and all of them gathered at the door. A large crowd followed the conscripts and gendarmes. They were, for the most part, the curious, men, women, and children. They watched wide-eyed and at a distance as two young Indians—the conscripts—came forward on foot, roped by the waist to the saddles of the mounted gendarmes. After each conscript came his family, weeping. The sergeant halted at the door of the subprefecture, dismounted, came to attention before the Draft Commission, and saluted.

"We've brought two, Your Excellency," he announced loudly, addressing the subprefect.

"They're conscripts?" asked Luna sternly.

"No, Excellency. They're enlistees."

The subprefect asked another question, which no one heard because of the clamor of the crowd. He raised his voice imperiously:

"Who are they? What are their names?"

"Isidoro Yépez and Braulio Conchucos, Excellency."

A path opened in the press of people and a very feeble old
man, covered to the ears by his huge straw hat, a poncho
folded on his shoulder, pants and shirt in tatters, holding one
of his sandals, came up to the subprefect.

"Dear master! Taita!" he cried, wringing his hands piteously. "Turn my Braulio loose! Turn him loose, I beg you,
taita!"

Two other Indians, about fifty years old, wearing ponchos
and weeping, and three barefoot women, their shawls pinned
at their breastbones by long cactus thorns, abruptly fell on
their knees before the members of the Draft Commission.

"Why, why, taitas? Why Isidoro? Dear masters, turn him
loose! Turn him loose!"

The three Indian women—the grandmother, mother, and
sister of Isidoro Yépez—sobbed and pleaded from their knees.
Braulio Conchucos' father came closer and kissed the subprefect's hand. The other two Indians—Isidoro's father and
uncle—made their way back to Isidoro and put his hat on him.

Very quickly, it seemed, there were a lot of people in front
of the Subprefecture. One of the gendarmes got down off his
mount. The other two remained in their saddles, and beside
them stood the two "enlistees," each attached to the mule of
each trooper. Braulio Conchucos was about twenty-three;
Isidoro Yépez, maybe eighteen. Both were sharecroppers from
Guacapongo. This was the first time they had ever been to
Colca. Illiterate, and without the slightest connection to the
economic or political affairs of Colca, they lived, so to speak,
outside the Peruvian state, outside the life of the nation. Their
only relation to it was confined to whatever services peasants
were normally forced to render to entities or persons wholly

invisible to them: digging irrigation ditches; clearing tracts of wilderness; carrying on their backs rocks, logs, or heavy sacks of grain without any idea where they were carrying them; driving trains of burros or mules laden with packs and boxes containing God knows what; leading yokes of oxen into fallow fields and dragging four-man threshers into great cocks of unthreshed wheat; tending irrigation valves all night long; saddling and unsaddling animals; reaping alfalfa and barley; grazing vast drifts of pigs, herds of horses, droves of oxen; shouldering the litters of foreign personages, very rich and very cruel; going down into mineshafts; being punched in the face and kicked in the kidneys; doing time in jail; making rope or peeling huge mounds of potatoes while manacled and chained; constantly suffering from hunger and thirst; going around almost naked; seeing their wives dragged off to be used at the pleasure of their overseers; chewing a plug of moistened coca leaves or a bit of raw cane or sipping a little chicha . . . And then being drafted or "enlisted," which is to say, brought by force to Colca, to do their compulsory military service. What did these two sharecroppers know of *compulsory military service?* What did they know of fatherland, government, public order, or national security? National security!—what was that? Who had the job of maintaining it, and who was going to enjoy it? All that the natives knew was that they were wretched and had no security. And as for being drafted or "enlisted," they knew only that from time to time the soldiers would sweep through the barrancas and into the huts in a vile temper, and tie the youngest Indians to the cruppers of their mules and take them away, slapping and yanking them as they trotted off. Where were they being taken? Nobody knew. And for how long? No Indian conscript or "enlistee" ever returned to his own region. Did they die on foreign soil of unknown diseases? Or did perhaps other soldiers or nameless sergeants kill them? Did they get lost, perhaps, somewhere in the world, abandoned on some lonely back road? Were they ever happy? No. There was little chance of that. Peasants could never be happy. The young Indians who left, never to return, were utterly, utterly wretched.

Braulio Conchucos' only family were his old father, a sister of ten, and a little brother of eight. His mother had died of typhoid. Two older brothers had also died in the epidemic which, four or five years before, had destroyed many people in and around Cannas. Braulio was in love with Barbara, the daughter of local cowherds from Guacapongo, and he planned to make her his wife. When the soldiers fell on Braulio's hut at five in the morning, still dark out, the children were terrified and began to cry. Their father, as he was about to leave, following his "enlisted" son, said to them,

"Go on over to Barbara's! They'll give you some breakfast. Go on! Don't stay here! Go along! I'll come back soon! With Braulio! I'll be back! I'll be back!"

The children clung desperately to the legs of Braulio and the old man, crying,

"No, no, papa! Don't go! Don't leave us! Don't go!"

One of the soldiers grabbed them by the arms and easily pulled them off. But as the men got ready to mount up, the children again threw themselves on Braulio and the old man, sobbing wildly and not letting them budge. The father pulled them away as he consoled them.

"All right, all right, it's okay. Hush! Now go on, go along to Barbara's."

Braulio would have dearly loved to embrace them but his hands were tied behind his back.

The sergeant, at last in his saddle, shouted angrily,

"Okay, move it, you stupid asshole! Start walking and no more fucking around."

The procession set out. The sergeant trotted into the lead. Then came one gendarme, with the conscript Isidoro Yépez on foot and tied to his mule, and then the other gendarme, and beside him, Braulio Conchucos, also on foot and leashed to his mount. With an abrupt and vicious jerk he pulled the rope taut so that Braulio would have fallen to the ground had he not been tied with so short a tether to the animal's neck, and Braulio now began to run at the mule's faster gait. Bringing up the rear of the detail rode a third gendarme, smoking a cigar. And behind him trailed the families of the "enlistees."

The moment Braulio's mule had started up the road, Braulio, almost with his first step and pulled as he was by his ropes, went flying against his brother and sister, knocking them down. Braulio had stumbled against his little sister's belly. She lay sprawled there a few moments, the wind knocked out of her. The boy picked himself up again, befuddled and half blinded, and began to follow Braulio and his father at a distance. Several times in the darkness, he tripped on the stones of the narrow road, pricking himself on cactus and bramble. The sound of the mules quickly began to fade. The boy halted and stopped crying so he could hear. Complete silence reigned all around the hut. The wind blew a moment in the amaranths that grew beside the well. The little girl, coming to her senses, started to cry, screaming,

"Papa! Papa! Papa! Braulio! Juan!"

The boy Juan went running back to the hut. The two children climbed the firepit, bundled up in their straw bedding, and again started to cry. The silhouettes of the soldiers, slapping the old man and Braulio and tying up the latter with shouts and curses, were fixed, as it were, on the children's retinas. Who were those monsters decked out in so many glittering buttons and carrying shotguns? Where did they come from? At what hour had they fallen on the hut? And why had they come for Braulio and their father? And beaten them, rained blows and kicks on them? Why? Were they men too, those soldiers, like other men? Juan thought not, but his sister, swallowing her tears, said,

"Yes, they're the same as anybody. Like papa, and like Braulio. I saw their faces. And their arms too, and their hands. One of them pulled my ears though I didn't do anything to him."

The little girl started to sob again, and Juan, a little scared and a little irritated, said to her,

"Hush up! Stop your crying, or they'll come back for us . . . hush now! They're devils—they have belts studded with jewels, they have round, pointed heads. They're going to come back, you'll see!"

"They talk like everybody else. They said, 'Asshole! You're not going to get away! Old shit! Walk! Son of a bitch!' They're dressed like shitty burros. They're awful strong. Did you see which way they went?"

"They went off through the cave, to the highroad. They'll come back, you'll see! They've come out of the cave. Mama said so. They leave the cave on whinnying mules with spurs and whips and their feet are lit up with little torches!"

"You're making it up! Mama didn't say that. They're Christians, like us. You'll see, tomorrow they'll come back again and you'll see that they're Christians. You'll see!"

Juan and his sister fell silent. But they went on wondering to themselves why Braulio and their papa had been taken away. Where were they being taken? Would the soldiers set them free again? When? What would they do to them? And the little girl said, by way of reassuring herself,

"And the others? The men and women who were with them? Don't you see? *They're* Christians! I know what I'm saying!"

"The others?" argued Juan in his usual way, agitated and apprehensive. "Yes, the others are Christians. But they're not their friends. They pulled them out of their huts just like they did Braulio and papa. You'll see, they'll throw them all in the cave. Before dawn! They have their palace there, with some devils as kings. They have parties. They send for people to serve the kings and live there all the time. Some escape but almost all of them die inside there. When they get old, they throw them in the fire and burn them alive. One got away one time and told his family everything . . ."

His sister had fallen asleep. Juan went on thinking about the soldiers for a long time, and when day broke, he began to feel cold, and he too fell asleep.

Guacapongo was a long way from Colca. In order to get back by 11 A.M., the soldiers had to move fast, often at a trot.

The families of the "enlistees" constantly lagged behind. But the two men themselves, like it or not, maintained the same pace as the animals. At first they pushed on without strain. But a few kilometers further on, they began to flag. They did not have the stamina to keep up with the mules. They were fluent and tireless runners, these Indians, but this time the ordeal was too great.

The road from Guacapongo to Colca continually varied in width, roughness, and direction, but in general it was narrow and stony, walled in by cactus and boulders, and for most of its length it meandered through sharp switchbacks, blind curves, steep grades, and sudden ravines. Two rivers, the Patarati and the Huayal, ran through this region; there were no bridges. The spring had been dry, but the waters of the Huayal flowed all year long, and here the force of its passage always made it difficult and risky to cross.

A terrible pace was enforced on both the animals and the conscripts. Again and again the soldiers dug their spurs into the mules and lashed them at every dig. There was no let-up, in spite of the sharp turns and sudden obstacles of the route. While it was still dark the animals bucked and reared again and again, struggling to avoid or jump over a drop-off, a mud hole, a stream that flooded the road, or whatever barrier. In a rage the sergeant buried his spurs to the shank in the ribs of his stalled mount and crossed its ears and flanks with lashes, swearing a blue streak. Finally he dismounted, drew from his rawhide saddlebag a bottle of brandy, took a long swig, and commanded the other troopers to do likewise. Then he called out to the straggling relatives and made them push the animal. At last the mules were forced to move on. After a nerve-wracking drumming of hooves, after sinking almost to their chests, they got out again to the other side of the road. And the "enlistees," how did they get over the bad places? Like the animals—except that they did not offer the least resistance. The first time they came to the foot of a steep escarpment on which there was not even the hint of a trail, Isidoro Yépez dared to say to the soldier he was tied to,

"Careful, taita! We're going to fall off!"

"Shut up, asshole!" answered the soldier, slapping him hard across the face.

It drew a little blood from Isidoro Yépez. From that moment on, the two "enlistees" sank into total silence. The soldiers were soon drunk. The sergeant wanted to get to Colca as soon as possible because at eleven o'clock he had a game of craps with his friends in the barracks. The Indians who followed Yépez and Conchucos disappeared now and again from the procession because, familiar with the terrain and going on foot, they left the highroad to make better time, taking short cuts by cutting across the fields. They did it by clambering up outcroppings, skirting the huge slabs, negotiating the ridges of ravines like mountain goats, or crossing a river by leaping from stone to stone or by trying their balance along a fallen tree.

During the crossing of the Huayal, just after daybreak, Braulio Conchucos felt himself at the point of dying. The sergeant crossed first, overcoming the fierce resistance of his mule; next came the soldier who led Isidoro Yépez. When the second soldier's mule found itself in the midst of the current, it lost its footing and was swept downstream a ways by the force of the water. It was submerged almost to the withers. The rider's legs were underwater and his anxiety was extreme.

He urged the animal on, screaming at it, whipping it. Isidoro, the water up to his chest, seemed calm and impassive in the face of the danger.

"Get out, motherfucker!" the soldier yelled at him, gripped by terror. "Keep going! Get out of the water! Hold on to the mule, hold on! Keep going! Don't let it drag you!"

From one side to the other the other soldiers shrieked in fear and ran about crazily, seeing the current about to capsize the mule and carry it downstream along with the soldier and his prisoner. Only Braulio, in the midst of the dangerous waters, and Isidoro Yépez, on the other side of the Huayal, remained silent, clear-headed, calm. Conchucos' guard, beside himself as his terror welled up, could do nothing but go on flogging Braulio savagely. Conchucos, trussed up tight, began to bleed but did nothing to extricate himself from his peril nor uttered a word in protest. Isidoro Yépez had been punched merely for mentioning the risks of the route. Why then say or do anything? These sharecroppers understood all too well their situation and their fate. They were nothing in themselves and could do nothing, whereas the soldiers could do everything and were everything. Then, too, Braulio Conchucos that morning had lost, in a single moment, all interest in life, had emptied himself of all feeling. To see the soldiers coming into one's hut in the night, to be beaten up and tied with ropes, and to feel oneself lost forever—it was all the same. They would carry him off to God knows where, like all the other young serfs, never to be set free. What difference would it make, to die by drowning or by some other evil chance? Moreover, Braulio Conchucos and Isidoro Yépez soon felt toward the soldiers a wordless and boiling hatred. Dimly they realized that to whatever extent these soldiers were mere instruments, executors of a will they knew nothing of and could not even imagine, they nevertheless contributed, in their cruelty and caprice, something peculiarly their own. Braulio Conchucos took a secret satisfaction in the soldier's fear. And if the waters swept them all away, well and good! Did not Braulio see at this very moment the water carrying off the blood that ran from his mouth? He then felt the whip across his face, again and again, and couldn't see any more. One eye was already swollen shut. He shivered from head to toe. For a moment, mule and conscript bobbed like uprooted stalks at the mercy of the current. But the soldier, crazed with terror, went on plying the lash with all his strength, the blows raining down on the heads of Braulio and the mule.

"Goddamn it!" shouted the soldier, struggling ashore. "Come on, mule! Go, you piece of shit, go, go!"

With a last desperate lunge the animal managed to make it to the other bank of the Huayal, bearing its double load of soldier and Conchucos. The march resumed. The sun grew scorching. Across the Huayal, the road ended in a long, endless slope. But the sergeant only dug in his spurs all the harder and brandished his whip more vigorously. Step by step the animals plodded upward, without halting, and beside them, the two "enlistees." Only now and then did the company halt.

"You some kind of smart-ass, stopping like that?" the soldiers yelled at the peasants. "Keep going, asshole! Just keep going and don't lean on the mules! Keep moving or I'll whip you within an inch of your life!"

The conscripts and the animals sweated and gasped for breath. The hides of the mules were matted, swirling in a thousand tangled kinks and ringlets. Sweat poured from their chests and flanks. They chewed at their bridles, foam cascading from their mouths. Their front hooves slipped on the rocks or, immobilized a moment, they trembled, retching and bending low. Their heads were stretched long at that moment, the ears thrown back, till their lower lips scraped the ground. Their nostrils flared wider than seemed possible, red, burnt dry. But the fatigue of Yépez and Conchucos was greater still. Both of them, beardless, their cotton shirts black with grime, hatless under the inflamed sun, bare calloused feet on the ground, arms tied behind them, rawhide thongs around their waists and tied to the necks of the mules, stained with blood— Conchucos with one eye swollen shut and welts all over his face—the "enlistees" mounted the hill, falling and dragging themselves back up. Falling? They could not even fall. At the hill's crest, their drained, exhausted bodies lost their last reserves and they let themselves be dragged, inert as sticks or stones, by the mules. Their will crushed by overwhelming fatigue, nerves deadened, muscles limp, knees and elbows powerless, heart numbed by the heat and the exertion of four straight hours on the march, Braulio Conchucos and Isidoro Yépez were little more than two pieces of human meat, more dead than alive, dragged every which way and sometimes hanging almost in mid-air. A cold sweat soaked them. Bloody froth oozed from their open mouths. Yépez began to give off a foul and nauseating odor. Something yellow ran down his ankles. Slack with mortal exhaustion, his functions out of control, the conscript was befouling himself with excrement.

"This asshole's shitting himself!" yelled his guard, and he held his nose.

The troopers burst out laughing and dug their spurs in harder.

When the curious came up to Isidoro Yépez in front of the Subprefecture of Colca, they laughed too, and then immediately backed away, pulling out their handkerchiefs. But when they approached Braulio Conchucos, they stood there for a long time inspecting his agonized and disfigured face. Some of the village women were angered and muttered words of protest. The crowd quickly grew noisy and agitated. The soldiers, before entering Colca, had washed off Conchucos' face in an irrigation ditch, but the contusions and the swollen eye were all the more obvious. Moreover, the soldiers had revived the captives by plunging their heads into cold water for a while, and for that reason Yépez and Conchucos were able to rouse a little from their stupor and make it into town on foot.

"The soldiers have beaten them!" the crowd shouted. "Look at their faces! They're bleeding! What a shameless crime! Pigs! Bandits! Murderers!"

Many people in Colca were crackling with fury. Pity and revulsion spread to every corner of town. The wave of collective anger rolled to the very foot of the Draft Commission. The subprefect Luna, stepping toward the sidewalk, hurled a furious shout over the assemblage:

"Silence! What do you want? What's all the ruckus about? Why these accusations?"

Parga, the mayor, came up to him.

"Pay no attention, my dear Subprefect," said he, taking him by the arm. "Come, come with us . . ."

"No, no!" Luna growled vehemently, roaring drunk from the brandies he had swallowed with the Marino brothers.

He steadied himself as best as he could at the sidewalk's edge and said to the sergeant, who stood in front of him awaiting his orders,

"Bring me the enlistees! Get them in here!"

"Very good, Your Excellency," the sergeant replied and passed the order on to the soldiers.

The prisoners were cut loose from the necks of the mules and brought into the office of the Draft Commission. Their arms still bound behind their backs, restrained by the rawhide thongs around their waists, Yépez and Conchucos stumbled forward in agony, shoved and jolted by their guards. The crowd, seeing them purple with bruises, mute, heads bowed, bodies half-fainting, agonized, shuddered in a single spasm of protest.

"Murderers!" men and women shrieked. "Look at them, almost dead! Half dead! Beasts! Murderers!"

The kinsfolk wanted to follow the conscripts into the sub-prefect's office, but the soldiers barred their way.

"Get back!" cried the sergeant with muffled anger, drawing his sword menacingly.

Once Yépez and Conchucos were inside, a cordon of soldiers, rifles at port, closed off the entrance to everyone else, and aimed at the crowd a steady stream of threats, obscenities, and insults.

"Animals! Swine! You don't know what the hell you're talking about! Idiots! You're all a bunch of mules. You don't know your ass from a hole in the ground! Dumb, filthy hicks!"

Most of the soldiers were from the coastal regions, and it was from this height that they thus expressed themselves to the mountain folk. In Peru the coastal people feel an intense and withering contempt for mountain people, highlanders, and the mountain people repay this scorn with raw, unspoken hatred.

Packed around the door of the Subprefecture and held back by the soldiers' rifles, the mob bubbled with growing indignation, which exploded into a stormy exchange between the troops and the people.

"Why did you beat them that way? Why?"

"Because they tried to escape. Because they attacked us from their huts with stones. Savages! Criminals!"

"No, no, you're liars!"

"Okay, then, because I felt like it."

"Murderers! Why do you take them prisoner?"

"Because I feel like it."

"Conscripts my ass! The very next thing, they get carried off to work on the plantations and in the mines, and then get their wages and land and livestock stolen from 'em! You're all nothing but thieves!"

A soldier shouted furiously,

"Enough, asshole! Shut up! Or I'll let you have it!"

He raised his rifle and made as if he were about to fire at random into the crowd, which responded to the threat with a great roar. Mayor Parga appeared at the door of the office.

"Gentlemen!" said he with the judicious and ceremonial air with which he disguised his fear. "What is this? What's the matter? Calm down! Take it easy, gentlemen."

Just then an ordinary man stepped from the crowd, descending upon the mayor, and deeply stirred yet full of energy, said to him,

"Your Honor! The people are anxious to see how this will be decided, and they ask . . ."

The soldiers grabbed him by the arms and covered his

mouth to keep him from going on, but the shrewd old mayor of Colca commanded that he be allowed to speak.

"The people, sir, call for justice!"

"Yes! Yes! Yes!" chorused the multitude. "Justice! Punishment for the ones who beat them up! Punishment for the murderers!"

The mayor blanched.

"Who are you?" He bent down to question this man who had spoken so fearlessly. "Come along, come into the office. Come in and we'll talk."

The man from the crowd entered the office. But who was this man of extraordinary boldness, to see to it that the rights of citizens were observed? Popular action in the face of the authorities was not exactly an everyday affair in Colca. The subprefect, the mayor, the judge, the doctor, the priest, the gendarmes enjoyed an unlimited freedom in the exercise of their duties. Neither the censure of public opinion nor any form of social pressure ever interfered with these functionaries in Colca. Not only that, but the most scandalous and abominable abuses of power generally aroused in the people nothing more than a vague, dark, diffuse, and altogether sentimental uneasiness. Immunity for administrative and official crimes was time-honored and routine in the history of the province. But here and now something new and unprecedented was happening. The case of Yépez and Conchucos was a violent shock to the mass of people, and a man from their ranks had dared to raise his voice, demanding justice and defying the wrath and vengeance of the authorities. Who was this man?

He was Servando Huanca, a blacksmith. Born in the mountains of the north, on the banks of the Marañón, he had

been living in Colca only about two years. He led an unusual
life. No woman, no kin, no amusements, very few friends. A
loner, he secluded himself at his forge from morning to night,
roasting. He was a type of pure Indian: high cheekbones, cop-
pery skin, small eyes deep-set and glittering, straight black
hair, medium height, and a reserved, almost taciturn de-
meanor. He was about thirty years old. He was one of the first
of those curious bystanders who had gathered around the soldiers and their captives. And he was also the first to cry out on
behalf of the latter in front of the Subprefecture. The others
had been afraid to stand up against this outrage. Servando
Huanca gave them courage, making himself the leader and
inspiration of the movement. In other days, while he was living among the sugar cane plantations of the Chicama Valley,
working as a mechanic, he had been both witness and participant in similar public demonstrations against the brutality of
overseers. Those events and hard experience gathered in the
various industrial centers to which he drifted, earning a living,
kindled in him a growing anger and grief over human injustice.
Huanca felt that his personal interests entered into this grief
and anger only to a small degree. Personally he had rarely
suffered abuse at the hands of those above him. But the brutal-
ities he saw committed daily against other workingmen and
other wretched Indians were extraordinary and innumerable.
Servando Huanca grieved, then, and raged against the bosses
or civil authorities more out of solidarity or, if you will, human-
ity, than out of any personal motive. He also became aware of
the social and comradely nature of his pain in the face of
injustice, through having discovered it equally in the other
workers when they talked among themselves of crimes and

abuses committed against the rest. Finally, Servando Huanca came, at various times, to join with his companions of work and pain in little guilds or rudimentary unions, and there he was given newspapers and pamphlets in which he read of cases and controversies touching on that injustice he knew so well and on the methods that those who suffer it should use to struggle against it and to abolish it from the earth. He was convinced that it was essential to protest injustice constantly and fiercely, whatever form it took. From then on, day and night, his wounded and single-minded spirit mulled over these ideas, this determination to resist. Could Servando Huanca now be said to possess class consciousness? Was he aware of it? His only tactic in the struggle came down to two very simple things: a union of those who suffer social injustice, and practical mass action.

"Who are you?" Subprefect Luna asked crossly, seeing Huanca enter his office just ahead of Mayor Parga.

"It's the blacksmith Huanca," answered Parga, soothing the subprefect. "Let him in! Don't worry. He wants to have a look at the conscripts, he claims they're dead and there's been some abuse . . ."

Luna interrupted, turning in exasperation toward Huanca:

"Abuse, my ass, you punk! Slob of a half-breed! Get the hell out of here!"

"It's all right, my dear Subprefect," the mayor broke in again. "Let him be. I beg you, leave him alone. He wants to see what condition the conscripts are in. Let him see them! Here they are, have a look."

"Yes, Subprefect," the blacksmith calmly joined in. "The

people demand it. I have been sent by those people outside."

Dr. Riaño, challenged in his liberalism, intervened.

"Very well," he said ceremoniously. "You are within your rights, since the people demand it. Subprefect," he said pompously, turning back to Luna, "I think that this man may proceed here. It doesn't inconvenience us in any way. The session of the Draft Commission can, in my judgment, continue. Let's take up the case of these enlistees."

"My feeling exactly," said the mayor. "Let's not waste time, Subprefect. I have things to do . . ."

The subprefect thought it over a moment, looked again at the judge and at the landowner, Iglesias, and at last agreed.

"All right," he said. "The session of the Draft Commission will continue."

Everyone took up his position once more. At one end of the office were Isidoro Yépez and Braulio Conchucos, guarded by two gendarmes and still restrained by the ropes around their waists. The troopers were cadaverously pale. They watched whatever went on around them with remote eyes and an icy, death-like indifference. Braulio Conchucos was extremely exhausted. He was having trouble breathing. His arms and legs were trembling. His head sank low, like the head of a dying man. At times he sagged and would have collapsed had not the guards held him and supported almost his full weight.

Servando Huanca stopped next to the two peasants, hat in hand, disturbed, yet quiet and resolute.

As soon as all the members of the Draft Commission were seated, a deafening outcry came from the plaza. The cordon of soldiers posted at the door responded to the mob with a storm of threats and insults. The sergeant leaped to the sidewalk and slashed with his sword as hard as he could at the front of the crowd.

"Assholes!" he howled, frothing with rage. "Get back! Back! Back!"

With a snarl Subprefect Luna commanded:

"Sergeant, restore order—I don't care how you do it. I give you full authority."

A long sob burst forth from the doorway. There were three Indian women, the grandmother, mother, and aunt of Isidoro Yépez, beseeching from their knees with clasped hands to be allowed to enter. The soldiers drove them back with feet and rifle butts.

Luna, presiding over the session, was speaking:

"And so, gentlemen, as you see, the troops have just brought the two enlistees from Guacapongo. Let's proceed then, in accordance with the law, to examine the case of these men, so that we may declare them ready to leave for the state capital in the next body quota from the province. First, Mr. Secretary, read what the Law of Compulsory Military service has to say about enlistees."

The secretary Boado read from a green booklet:

"Title IV—Concerning Enlistees—Article 46: All Peruvian males who are between the ages of nineteen and twenty-two years and who have not fulfilled their obligation to register themselves for Compulsory Military Service in their respective districts will be considered enlisted. Article 47: Enlistees will, immediately upon being taken into custody, be compelled by force to perform their military service, and will not be allowed to appeal or to avail themselves of any of the rights, exceptions, or extenuating circumstances extended to conscripts in general and contained in Article 29, Title II, of this Law. Article 48—"

"Enough!" Judge Ortega interrupted loudly. "I don't see any point in reading the rest of the law, since all the members of the Commission know it by heart. I suggest that the secretary check the military registration rolls and see if the names of these men appear there."

"One moment, Dr. Ortega," argued Mayor Parga. "It will be useful to know first the ages of these enlistees."

"Yes," the subprefect chimed in. "Let's see," he went on, speaking paternally to Isidoro Yépez. "You, how old are you? First, what's your name?"

Isidoro Yépez seemed to be emerging from a dream, and he responded in a weak and nervous voice.

"My name is Isidoro Yépez, taita."

"How old are you?"

"Well, I don't know, taita. Twenty, or twenty-four, who knows, taita?"

"Don't know? What's with this 'don't know'? Come on! Tell me, how old are you? Speak! Tell the truth."

"He doesn't even know himself," said Dr. Riaño, with a kind of pitying disgust. "They're really ignorant. Don't press him, Subprefect."

"All right," Luna went on, looking at Yépez. "Did you write your name in the military registry?"

The peasant's eyes grew wide, trying to take in what Luna was saying, and he answered, in a singsong way,

"Wrote down, taita, in your write-up?"

The subprefect repeated his question, nearly shouting:

"Animal! Don't you know what I'm talking about? Tell me if you signed up!"

At this point Servando Huanca intervened.

"Gentlemen!" said the blacksmith with quiet force. "This man is a poor, ignorant native. You can see that. He is illiterate. Wretched. Confused. He doesn't know how old he is. He doesn't know if he is registered or not. He doesn't know anything, anything at all. How can you take him as an enlistee when nobody has ever told him that he had to register or given him any notice, nor does he know what military registration is, or the country, or the state, or the government?"

"Silence!" Judge Ortega shouted angrily, interrupting Huanca and heaving himself violently to his feet. "Enough of this nonsense!"

At that moment, Braulio Conchucos' body stiffened, and after a few convulsions, he suddenly slumped and hung motionless in the arms of his guard. Dr. Riaño went over to him, tried briefly to revive him, and said with professional briskness,

"He's dead."

Braulio Conchucos sagged slowly to the floor.

Servando Huanca leapt between the gendarmes and out to the street, crying savagely to the crowd in a voice that was hoarse with rage:

"One of them is dead! He's dead! The soldiers have killed him! Down with the subprefect, down with the authorities! Long live the people!"

A spasm of collective fury at once passed through the crowd.

"Down with the murderers!" the people howled. "Let the butchers die!"

The confusion, turmoil, and terror were instantaneous. There was an abrupt and fierce collision between the crowd and the troops. The subprefect's voice could be heard clearly, issuing orders,

"Fire, sergeant! Open fire!"

The fusillade into the crowd was heavy, long, and very bloody. The people, unarmed and taken by surprise, defended themselves with paving-stones, and some surged into the Subprefecture. Most fled, aghast. Here and there lay many bodies, fallen dead or wounded. There was dust and smoke everywhere. Doors slammed shut all over the plaza. Gradually the rifle fire thinned out to a few scattered shots.

All this took only a few seconds. When it was over, the police were still masters of the city. They circled the plaza, inflamed, firing at random. Except for them and the dead or dying bodies strewn at intervals, the plaza was as empty as a desert. Beneath the beautiful, blazing midday sun, the clear blue air of Colca was saturated with blood and tragedy. A few buzzards circled above the roof of the church.

Dr. Riaño and the great landlord Iglesias gingerly emerged from a wine cellar. Little by little, a few curious people appeared at the edges of the plaza. José Marino was looking anxiously for his brother. Others asked after the fate of various people. Nervous inquiries were made about the subprefect, the judge, and the mayor. A moment later, all three, Luna, Ortega, and Parga, appeared on the street. The doors of houses and shops opened again. A hum of lamentation filled

the plaza. Around each corpse, each of the wounded, a commotion gathered. Although the clash was over, the troopers,
and especially the sergeant, went on firing their rifles. Both
the soldiery and the civil authorities seemed possessed by a
wild and ungovernable rage and they filled the air with venge-
ful shouts. Emerging from the scattered groups on the plaza
came various merchants, small shopkeepers, artisans, clerks,
and even the rich and powerful—old Iglesias at the head of
these—seeking out the subprefect and the other officials,
loudly condemning the rising of the rabble, declaring their
own loyalty, and offering their firm and unconditional support
in restoring public order.

"It was the Indians, just animals, just savages," the petits-
bourgeois of Colca cried indignantly.

"But somebody incited them," said others. "The rabble
are stupid and won't ever move on their own."

The subprefect ordered that the dead and wounded be
gathered up and that an official civil guard be formed immediately, made up of all citizens aware of their civic responsibili-
ties, with the avowed purpose of reorganizing the populace
together with the soldiery and reestablishing urban security.
So it was. At the head of this double army stood Subprefect
Luna, Mayor Parga, Judge Ortega, Dr. Riaño, the great
rancher Iglesias, the Marino brothers, Secretary Boado, the
priest Velarde, the justices of the peace, the schoolmaster,
the councilmen, the governor, and the police sergeant.

In this incursion into all the streets and back alleys of
Colca, the police took many prisoners, both men and women.
The subprefect and his cohorts went right into people's houses
and apartments, either with permission or by force, and one

by one arrested all whom they suspected of having participated in any way in the uprising. The authorities and the petits-bourgeois held the lower classes, that is to say, the Indians, responsible for everything that had happened. It was the beginning of a fierce and implacable repression against the common people. Aside from the police, a considerable number of citizens armed themselves with rifles and carbines, and almost all of the subprefect's entourage carried, with or without good reason, their pistols. With all this, no Indian accused of taking part in the trouble could escape punishment. A door would be splintered with a blow of a rifle butt, whereupon the frightened tenants would flee. Waving pistols, the righteous searched them out and hunted them down, over terraces and rooftops, in fireplaces and pig-hutches, under mounds of garbage, everywhere. In the end, they got them, dead or alive. From early afternoon, when the shooting started, till after midnight, they went on firing their weapons at people with never a pause. The most bloodthirsty in this repression were the judge Ortega and the priest Velarde.

"Here, my good Subprefect," growled the priest venomously, "here there is no room for anything but the iron fist. If you don't come down hard, that mob of Indians can get together again tonight and overpower Colca, looting, robbing, killing . . ."

At around twelve midnight, the staff of the civil guard, and at their head, Subprefect Luna, were assembled in a conference room in the City Hall. After an exchange of ideas among the principals gathered there, it was agreed to send a telegram describing the day's events to the State Prefecture. The text went like this: "Prefect, Cuzco. Today, 1:00 P.M. during ses-

sion provincial Draft Commission mutinous armed mob attacked Subprefecture stones and gunfire. Police restored order
respecting life and property of citizens. Twelve dead, eighteen
wounded, two policemen with serious injuries. Investigating
mob causes and aims. All social classes, authorities, entire
populace standing with me. Security complete. Will communicate result investigations hearings trials punishment of those
responsible unfortunate occurrence. Details by mail. (Signed)
Subprefect Luna."

Then Mayor Parga offered brandy to all present, along
with a brief toast.

"Gentlemen!" said he, glass in hand. "In the name of the
City Council, over which I have the honor to preside, I deplore the unpleasant incidents of this afternoon, and congratulate the Honorable Subprefect of this province for the vigor,
fairness, and decorum with which he has restored order, freedom, and civil peace in Colca. Likewise, on behalf of the
feelings and convictions of all the gentlemen present here—
worthy representatives of business, agriculture and public
administration—I beg Señor Luna to crack down ruthlessly on
the instigators, on all those responsible for the rebellion, in the
certainty that we will be most grateful and that the best people
of Colca stand behind him. Gentlemen! To our deliverer, the
Honorable Señor Luna, salud!"

A burst of applause greeted old Parga's speech and the
brandies were downed. The subprefect responded thus:

"Your Honor, deeply moved by the undeserved praise with
which you have drunk my health, I can offer only my apprecia-
tion. In truth, I have done nothing but my duty. I have pro-
tected the province from the outrages and excesses of an

angry, blind, ignorant mob. That is all I have done for you, gentlemen—nothing more. I too deplore what has happened. But I am determined to punish the guilty without favor or mercy. What the police have done so far is nothing. I will make these savages and animals understand that they cannot provoke the authorities without paying for it. I promise you they will be punished to the last man. Salud!"

The ovation Luna received was sonorous and manly, like his speech. Many embraced the mayor and the subprefect and congratulated them fervently. There was another round of drinks. Ortega, Velarde and Dr. Riaño also made speeches, all condemning the lower classes and demanding exemplary punishments for them. The Marino brothers and Iglesias the landowner, half in monologue, half in conversation, pleaded insistently for a ruthless repression of the Indians. Iglesias said vindictively,

"We must get the blacksmith; he's the cleverest and he's the one who incited the others. He must have gotten away. But he's got to be found and given a good beating, the son of a bitch!"

José Marino argued for worse:

"Beating, my ass! He needs a bullet in the gut! The creep! The crazy shit!"

"I think he was shot dead in the plaza," Boado suggested timidly.

The subprefect corrected him.

"No, he was the first to escape, at the first shot. But he must be captured. Sergeant!" he called in a loud voice.

The sergeant stepped up, came to attention, and saluted.

"Your Excellency!"

"You are to make an intensive search for the blacksmith. I want him taken regardless of the cost. Wherever he may be, he must be snapped up. Shoot him in the belly, that'll fix him. Sure! Do whatever you have to, just bring me his body. Your promotion to lieutenant is in the bag."

"Very good, Excellency," the sergeant answered happily. "Your orders will be obeyed. Have no fear."

From time to time pistol and carbine shots could be heard in the distance, breaking the silence of the night. They came from the bands of civil guards who were roving the city. In City Hall, the brandy went round and round, and the priest Velarde, Luna, and José Marino were beginning to show signs of drunkenness. A fat blue cloud of cigar smoke hung in the air. The meeting grew progressively merrier. From the topic of the uprising there soon flowed various wickedly amusing stories. In a group composed of the sergeant, a soldier, and a justice of the peace, the justice, tipsy and red-faced, exclaimed,

"What morons the Indians are!"

At which the sergeant said boastfully,

"Oh, did I fuck them! The second I saw that blacksmith leaping into the plaza yelling 'He's dead!' I turned to this old guy standing beside me and gave him a terrific crack on the head with my rifle—left him for dead. Then I backed up a little and began firing at the whole damned tribe—like a machine gun: bang bang bang bang! Fuck! I don't know how many I potted. But I do know I emptied my whole cartridge-belt, and all I saw was a cloud of dust and the fuckers running every which way . . . Oh, mama! I got me at least seven, all by myself, and that's not counting the wounded."

"You should have seen *me!*" cried the soldier proudly. "Shit! I didn't let them Indians so much as wiggle their asses. Before they even threw one stone, I got two of them, pow, right in front of me, point blank. One of them was a woman who had just been giving me that 'master, master' shit. Gave her a rifle butt in the belly, laid her out cold. The other was on his knees, blubbering and pleading, but I broke his ribs with one smash."

The justice of the peace listened to them with a horror he could scarcely conceal, in spite of which he expressed enthusiastic approval.

"Well done, well done! Stupid Indians! The one you really should have put holes in is that half-breed Huanca. Too bad you let him get away alive! Goddamn!"

"Ah," swore the sergeant, waving his hands, "that one? You'll see, you'll see soon enough how I deal with him. Just leave him to me! The subprefect told me if I bring in his corpse, I can count on being promoted to lieutenant."

But a more important conversation was unfolding that very moment between Luna and the Marino brothers. José Marino had beckoned Luna aside, grasping him warmly by the arm.

"Allow me, my dear Subprefect," he said. "I'd like to have a drink with you."

Mateo Marino poured the brandy and the three men went off to a corner, glass in hand.

"Now look," said José Marino in a low voice. "You know very well that I am your true friend, your friend forever. I've proven it many times. I've always felt the greatest, the most sincere affection for you. Many times, without your knowl-

edge—I don't like to tell anybody what I'm doing for him—
many times I have spoken with Mr. Taik and Mr. Weiss about
you. They have a high opinion of you. Oh, yes! I can tell. It's
clear to me that they're very pleased with you. *Very* pleased!
But some people here," he said, referring with a vague gesture
to the people gathered in the hall, "have written to
Mr. Taik repeatedly to badmouth you . . ."

"Yeah," said Luna, with a smug smile. "I've been told
about that. I knew it already."

"They've written, telling tales and making you look bad,
saying you're nothing but an agent of the deputy, Dr. Urteaga,
and all you do here is work for Urteaga against the interests of
the Mining Society."

The subprefect gave a bitter and malevolent smile. José
Marino went on, drawing himself to his full height and taking
on a protective tone.

"Naturally, I've defended you with all my might. And
there's even more. Mr. Taik was already pretty well taken in by
all that gossip, and one day I was called to his office and he
said to me, 'Señor Marino, I've brought you to my office so
that I could speak with you about a very serious and very
private matter. Sit down and answer my questions. How does
Subprefect Luna conduct himself with you people in Colca?
Please, I want you to be completely candid. Because people in
Colca have written to me so many things against Luna that,
quite frankly, I don't know what to believe. So I want you to
tell me honestly how Luna gets along with you. Does he lend
you every possible assistance in collaring workers? Does he
look out for your interests, is he one of you? Because the
Mining Society saw to it that Luna was named subprefect for

the sole purpose of ensuring that the police would do our bidding in anything that had to do with the workforce. You know this very well. The rest is of minor importance—that Luna is always hanging around with Urteaga's political pals, that he gets drunk in the wrong company, none of that matters to me.' That's what the gringo said. He was really worked up. I told him that you were okay with us, that we had nothing to complain of. 'Because,' the gringo says to me, 'if Luna doesn't accommodate you, I will inform our office in Lima immediately and have him dismissed the same day. You understand that this firm represents some very heavy investments in Peru and we're not about to let anyone endanger them.' That's how the gringo talked. But I told him that those rumors were not true and that you were with us one hundred percent."

"I know," said Mateo Marino, "I know who writes that stuff to the yanquis."

"Right, right," José chimed in warmly. "But the fact is that the yanquis already have a flea in their ear and we have to be careful . . ."

"But it's all lies!" cried Luna. "You, more than anyone, are witnesses to my absolute loyalty and my unconditional devotion to Mr. Taik!"

"Of course!" said José Marino, puffing himself up triumphantly. "That's exactly why I defended you, right down the line, and Mr. Taik said to me, 'Very well, Señor Marino, your word is good enough for me.' "

"Great, great!" said Mateo.

Very moved, Luna answered,

"I'm really very grateful to you, my dear Don José. And you know that I'm your sincere friend, ready to do anything I can for you. Just tell me what you want and I'll do it on the spot. On the spot! You know that!"

"Excellent, excellent!" said Mateo again. "Let's drink to that, Subprefect."

"Yes, to you!" José Marino raised his glass to Luna. "To our deep and noble friendship! Salud!"

"To that, and to Marino Brothers!" said the subprefect. "And Mr. Taik and Mr. Weiss! And the Mining Society! And to the United States! Salud!"

The three men had several more drinks. During one of these, José Marino asked the subprefect, privately and sotto voce as always,

"How many Indians have been taken prisoner today?"

"About forty."

José Marino was about to add something, but he checked himself. Finally he said,

"Do you remember what we said to you this morning about the workers?"

"Sure. That you need a hundred for the mines."

"Exactly. That's it. But I think we could do some business. Look—since you don't have enough gendarmes yet to chase after all our runaway peons right away, and since you don't know what to do with all those Indians in your jail, why not give some of them to us to send to Quivilca right now?"

"Ah, well," cried the subprefect, "you understand, that's not so easy. Because . . . but wait! Wait a minute . . ."

Luna pensively stroked his chin and finally said to José Marino in a low, conspiratorial voice,

"Say no more. It's settled. You have my word on it."

Mateo hurried off to get three more brandies.

"Gentlemen!" José raised his glass and announced loudly to everyone in earshot. "I propose a toast to the Honorable Roberto Luna, our good Subprefect, who has just saved us from the Indian horde. I can assure you, gentlemen, that the Government will know how to reward Señor Luna for what he has done for Colca today. And I propose that all of us present here sign a memorandum to the Minister of the Interior, expressing the gratitude that this province feels toward Señor Luna. And in addition I propose that a committee be named and given the job of organizing an homage to Señor Luna, with a great banquet and a gold medal, a gift from the sons of Colca."

"Bravo, bravo! Hip, hip, hurrah!"

So went the exuberant tumult in the municipal chambers. Judge Ortega, now very drunk, called one of the troopers over and said,

"Go bring musicians. Wake those half-breeds up any way you can, and tell 'em the subprefect, the judge, the mayor, the priest, all the best people of Colca, are here and to get over here immediately."

Dr. Riaño raised a scruple.

"Dr. Ortega, do you think we ought to have music?"

"But of course. Why not?"

"Because there were so many deaths today, and people are going to say . . ."

"What people? The Indians? That's a good one." And he turned back to the gendarme. "Go on, off with you."

And the gendarme took off running, to bring the music.

In the wee hours, the City Hall turned into a night club. The band played waltzes and marineras, and the revelry rose to a manic frenzy. Many had already gone off to bed but those who remained—a dozen or so—were blind drunk. Men danced with men. Father Velarde and Judge Ortega could not get enough of the marinera. The priest took off his cassock and set himself up as the life of the party. He danced and sang at the top of his lungs. Then he suggested they go to a house of some chicheras where he and Dr. Riaño had lecherous designs on two pretty Indian girls. But someone insisted that they couldn't go, because the father of these girls was one of those wounded in the plaza.

Holding one another by the arm, Mayor Parga, Subprefect Luna and the Marinos talked animatedly. Swaying drunkenly, the mayor babbled,

"The yanquis made me what I am. I owe everything to them, being mayor, everything. They're my heroes. They are the ones who count in Colca."

"Not only in Colca," Mateo put in, "but in the whole state! They give the orders. Goddamn! Long live Mr. Taik, gentlemen!"

Subprefect Luna, conversant as he was in international affairs, was lecturing grandly to his friends:

"Ah, gentlemen, the United States is the greatest nation on earth! What incredible progress, what wealth! Great men, the yanquis. Almost all of South America is in the hands of yanqui money—think of that! The biggest mining operations, the railroads, the rubber and sugar cane plantations, it's all being done with New York dollars. It's an amazing thing. And you'll see, the war in Europe's not going to end until the U.S. gets into it. Remember what I'm telling you. It's a sure thing.

What balls that Wilson has, what brains! And his speeches! I
read one the other day. Shit, no doubt about it . . ."

José Marino elaborated loudly:

"And most of all, the Mining Society. That's the biggest
mining operation in Peru! Copper mines in the north, gold
and silver in the center and in the south. All over the place!
Mr. Weiss told me in Quivilca what the Mining Society con-
sists of. That's some enormous outfit! I'll just tell you that the
partners of the Society are the biggest millionaires in the U.S.
Many of them are bankers and they're on the boards of a
thousand other corporations, mining, sugar, cars, oil! Mr. Taik
and Weiss, just between the two of them, have colossal fortunes . . ."

Leaning on Judge Ortega's arm, Father Velarde approached them, asking,

"All right, gentlemen, what's this all about?"

"At the moment," Mateo answered proudly, "we're talking
about the yanquis."

"Ah!" cried the priest. "The gringos are really something!
Let's drink to the North Americans, they're the ones who give
the orders. Shoot! I saw the bishop himself bow to Mr. Taik
the last time I was in Cuzco. The bishop wanted to change
priests in Canta, but Mr. Taik said no, and so Monsignor had
to knuckle under."

Mateo Marino issued a loud order to the musicians,

"An ataque, an ataque!"

The musicians, who were in the hallway and knew nothing of what was being talked about in the conference rooms,
launched into a energetic, rhythmic, slightly monotonous

piece. The racket was deafening and total confusion reigned—
everyone had a glass in his hand and was yelling at the same
time, cheering the United States, the Mining Society, the
North Americans, cheering Wilson, Mr. Taik, Mr. Weiss,
Quivilca, cheering the subprefect, the mayor, the judge, Señor
Iglesias, the Marino brothers, and damning the Indians in the
same breath.

In the midst of this din and punctuating the enthusiastic
notes of the music, several pistol shots rang out. Judge Ortega
and Father Velarde pulled out their handkerchiefs and began
to dance. Seeing them, the musicians slid without missing a
beat into the fugue of a contagious marinera. The others
formed a ring around them, clapping their hands and emitting
frantic and strident cries.

The sun began to peep from behind the far-off snowy
peaks of the Andes.

The next day, Dr. Riaño performed autopsies on the
corpses. Three of the wounded had died sometime during the
night. Some of the dead were buried that afternoon.

Subprefect Luna, still in bed around 1:00 P.M., found
among the morning's mail an answering telegram from the prefect, which went: "Subprefect Luna. Colca.—Deplore events,
congratulate posture on unlawful Indian riot and restoration
public order. (Signed) Prefect Ledesma." Luna then went on
to read his letters and newspapers. Suddenly, with a smile of
satisfaction, he called out to his orderly:

"Anticona!"

"Your Excellency."

"Go and call Señor José Marino. Tell him that I'm waiting for him and he's to come right away."

"Very well, Your Excellency."

In a few minutes José Marino entered the subprefect's bedroom, smiling contentedly.

"What's up? Did you sleep well?"

"Yes," said Luna with a weary wave of the hand. "Come in and sit down. The boozing always beats hell out of me. Old age, but what can you do?"

"Not me. I slept like a rock."

"Well, my dear Marino, I have just received a wire from the prefect. Look."

The subprefect held out the telegram and José Marino read it silently.

"Terrific!" he cried. "Terrific! You see? Just what I told you yesterday. Of course. The prefect and the minister have to be happy about how you've handled things. And I'm going to write directly to Mr. Taik, telling him what's happened and saying that he should immediately put in a good word for you to Cuzco and to Lima, so that yesterday's business will be approved and you won't be transferred from Colca."

"That's the ticket! Wonderful! I leave it in your hands. As for those Indians we arrested, I guess you could have, say, fifteen of them for the mines. You know, I just read in the paper that the United States is entering the war in Europe."

"Really?" asked José Marino, excited.

"Yes, really. I just read it in the paper."

"In that case, Mr. Taik must know about it by now and probably has already doubled the shifts in the mines. He has to send a big trainload of tungsten right away to Mollendo, to be shipped to New York."

"That's exactly why I called you, seeing as how the Mining Society needs laborers, to say you can have fifteen Indians today, if you want them—they're in the jail right now."

"What about twenty, can you do that?"

"For my part, I'd be happy to give you twenty. You know that I'm here to serve you and that's the only thing I care about. I know that as long as Mr. Taik is satisfied with me, I have nothing to worry about. But I told you yesterday that I need at least five conscripts before the end of the month. Of the Indians in the jail, I have to take three more to bring my force up to full strength. I can't look bad to the prefect. Put yourself in my place. Then, too, it's not a good idea to go too far in this business of supplying Indians for Quivilca. You can't trust Riaño and Iglesias. If old Iglesias finds out that I've given you twenty Indians for Quivilca, he'll want the same for his plantation, and the way he's always writing to Urteaga, he can make me look bad with the Government."

"But if we have Mr. Taik on our side . . ."

"Yeah, sure, but it's always wise to be on good terms with the deputy."

"No, no, I assure you, there's no reason old Iglesias should know about it. Quivilca is a long way off. Once the Indians are in the mines, nobody will know anything about them, where they are, what they're doing, nothing."

"What about their families? What if they go to Quivilca?"

"Okay, but you can keep it from them. See that they don't stir a foot or do anything. Then you tell everyone that the Indians were set free and must have run away later out of fear.

Do it that way, and then if it gets out that some of them are in the mines, you can say that those are the very ones who ran off to Quivilca because they were afraid of punishment for what happened yesterday."

And so it was agreed between José Marino and Subprefect Luna. That very night, after a selection of the most passive and ignorant, twenty Indians were slipped out of jail, three by three, in the hour before dawn. The town was sunk in utter silence. The streets were empty. With the Indians went two gendarmes, armed to the teeth, who led each threesome to the outskirts of Colca, on the road to Quivilca. There was assembled the complete group of twenty Indians that Luna had promised to Marino Bros., and at four o'clock in the morning, they set out for the tungsten mines. The twenty Indians had their arms bound behind their backs and all were tied together by a strong cable, single file. They were guarded by José and Mateo on horseback, a gendarme, and four trusted thugs on the Marinos' payroll. The seven guards carried pistols and carbines and plenty of ammunition.

In order to avoid chance encounters along the way, the prisoners were made to march mostly on narrow and little-used footpaths.

No one said anything to these Indians, either about where they were being carried off to, or for how long, or under what circumstances. The Indians submitted without a word. They stared at one another, understanding nothing, and shuffled slowly on, heads down, sunk in a woeful silence. Where were they being taken? To Cuzco maybe, to stand trial for the killings in Colca. But they hadn't done a thing! Then again, who knows? Or maybe they were on their way to be drafted. But could old men be drafted too? Maybe—who knows? And then, too, why were the Marinos with them, and other civilians, none of them in uniform? Could it be to help out the subprefect? Or possibly they were being taken to some horrible place, far away, to be abandoned, just because they happened to be grabbed in the plaza at the time of the shooting? But where might that place be, and why the idea of punishing them by losing them that way, so far from home? Who knows? Who knows? But not one handful of roasted kernels. Not one bit of wheat or barley meal. Not even a plug of coca leaves. When it was fully morning and the sun beginning to burn down, many of them were thirsty. But not a sip of chicha. Not a taste of cane liquor. Not even a drop of water. And their families? Poor Paula, pregnant. Santos, still such a little boy. Old Nico, left eating breakfast in the yard. Mama Dolores, so thin, the poor woman, and so good-hearted. And the yellow bell peppers, already huge. The pinch of maize, still green. And the grey cock, bound for Chuca. All, all left far behind . . . for how long? Who knows? Who knows?

PART 3

A few weeks later, the blacksmith Huanca was deep in conversation with Leónidas Benites and the timekeeper who had once been the lover of the dead Graciela. It was night. They were in the timekeeper's hut, in the worker's camp but on the farthest outskirts of Quivilca, near the ravines of Sal Si Puedes. In the one room of that wretched hut where the timekeeper lived alone, a kerosene lamp was burning next to the bed. For furniture, there was only a crude wooden bench and two camphor stumps to sit on. On the arched walls, papered with newsprint, various photos cut out of *Variedades* were stuck with gum. The three men talked in low voices, secretively. From time to time they fell silent and peered watchfully out past the cacti in the doorway toward the deserted road drowned in the silence of the plateau. What strange circumstance could have joined these men, each so different from the others, in a single setting? What extraordinary incident had so shaken Benites as to rouse him and draw him to the humble timekeeper and, more peculiar still, to Servando Huanca, the taciturn and seditious blacksmith? And how, too, had Huanca managed to turn up in Quivilca, after the bloody events in Colca?

"We're agreed, then?" Huanca asked with intensity.

Benites seemed hesitant, but the timekeeper replied with an air of deep conviction,

"I say yes. I'm completely convinced."

Servando Huanca turned insistently to Benites.

"Well, let's see, Señor Benites—you're not convinced that the gringos and the Marinos are thieves and criminals, and that they live and grow fat on the flesh and blood of the Indians?"

"Yes," said Benites, "completely convinced."

"Well, then? The same thing, the very same thing, is going on in every mine in every country on earth—in Peru, in China, in India, in Africa, in Russia . . ."

Benites interrupted,

"But not in the United States, or in England, France, or Germany, because there the working class, the poor people, are well off."

" 'The poor people are well off?' What kind of nonsense is that? If you're poor, you're not well off."

"I mean that the bosses of France and England and Germany and the United States aren't so bad, they don't exploit their own countrymen the way they do the natives in other countries."

"All right, all right. The French bosses and millionaires, yanqui, German, English, what you will, are worse thieves and criminals with the peasants of India, Russia, China, Peru and Bolivia, but they're greedy and murderous enough toward the lower classes in their own countries. Everywhere, and I mean everywhere, some men are bosses and others are workers, some men are rich and others poor. And the revolution, what it's after is to overthrow all the gringos and exploiters in the world and free the Indians everywhere. Have you read what they're saying in the newspapers, that the workers and peasants have risen up in Russia? They've risen up against the bosses and the rich, against the great landlords, and against the government, and overthrown them, and now there's another government . . ."

"Yes. Yes, I've read about it in *El Comercio*," said Benites. "But they rose only against the czar. Not against the bosses and rich landlords, because there are always bosses, always millionaires. All they overthrew was the czar."

"Yes, but just wait . . ."

"I know!" said Benites enthusiastically. "There's a great man in the new government whose name is . . . wait . . ."

"Kerensky," said Huanca.

"That's it, Kerensky. They say he's really smart, a great speaker, a patriot, and that he'll defend the rights of the workers and the poor."

Servando Huanca burst out laughing, mimicking him derisively:

"Defend their rights! Oh sure!"

"He will. He's bright, he's decent, and he's a true patriot."

"He'll be another czar, that's all," said the blacksmith heatedly. "The intellectuals never do anything worth a damn. The ones who are clever but not really for the working class, for the poor, all they know how to do is get ahead and establish themselves in the government and then they too grow rich and forget about the needy and the working people. When I was

working on the sugar plantations around Lima, I read that
right now there's only one man on earth, his name is Lenin,
that he's the only intellectual who is truly with the workers
and the poor, who is working to defend them against the criminal bosses and landowners. Now that's a great man. And
you'll see. He's a Russian, I hear, and the bosses in every
country can't even stand to see his picture, and they're after
their governments to hunt him down and shoot him."

The surveyor was incredulous.

"He won't do anything either. What's he going to do if
they hunt him down and shoot him?"

"You'll see. I have a newspaper here that was sent to me
secretly from Lima, and it says that Lenin is going to Russia
and that he's going to stir up the masses against that Kerensky
and overthrow him and put the workers and the poor in power.
And it also says that the same thing has to be done everywhere, here in Peru, and in Chile, and abroad, in every country, to kick the gringos and bosses out and take over the
government ourselves, the workers and the poor!"

Benites smiled skeptically. The timekeeper, on the other
hand, listened to the blacksmith with fervor.

"Ah," said Benites with a worried air, "that's not so easy.
Poor Indians and laborers can't make a government, they don't
even know how to read. They're still ignorant. And beyond
that, there are two things we mustn't forget: first, that the
working class without the intellectuals—without lawyers, doctors, engineers, priests, teachers—can do nothing, and won't
be able to do anything, and never will be able! And second,
even if the workers were prepared to govern, they would always have to take a back seat to those who put up the capital,
because all the workers have to offer is their labor."

"All right, but let's understand each other, Señor Benites. I've already told you that . . ."

"Yes, we agree. We're agreed that the only people who should govern . . ."

"No, no, no! Wait a minute, please, let me say something! Let's speak in turn. You say that the workers can't accomplish anything without lawyers, teachers, doctors, priests, engineers. Okay. But what happens is that the priests and teachers and lawyers and so forth are the first to exploit the Indians and the peons and steal from them."

"No, sir! No, sir!"

"Yes, sir! Yes!" replied the blacksmith passionately.

"Yes, yes!" the timekeeper echoed him impulsively. "The doctors and engineers and all those who take themselves for clever young fellows, they're just thieves, always finding ways to fleece the Indians and the poor. Yes! You yourself," the timekeeper went on irritably, leaning closer to the surveyor, "you yourself and Zavala the schoolmaster and the engineer Rubio were all involved in Graciela's death in the store!"

"No, sir, you're wrong!" replied Benites nervously.

"Yes! Yes!" cried the timekeeper defiantly. "You're a hypocrite, and the only reason you've come to see Huanca is to get back at Marino and the gringos for taking away your job and cutting you off from your pals, no other reason. You and Rubio were the first to jump on Marino's bandwagon, swindling the Soras out of their farms and animals and corn, robbing them and then sending them down into the mines to die like dogs among the machines and the dynamite. And now you want to take us in and say you're on our side when you're not. You're going to go running back to the gringos and the Marinos as soon as they call you and offer you another job. And then you'll be the first to sell us out and tell the bosses everything we're doing and saying here. That's right! That's how engineers are, and teachers and doctors and priests, the whole bloody lot of you! We can't believe a word you say. Thieves! Turncoats! Hypocrites! Shameless bastards!"

"All right, that's enough! Quiet down!" Huanca spoke affectionately to the timekeeper, coming between him and Benites. "Let it be. There's nothing to be gained talking like that. Let's keep calm. No confusion, no uproar. A revolutionary ought to be calm."

"Besides," said Benites, pale and beseeching, "I haven't done any of those things. I swear to you on my mother that I wasn't involved in any way in the Indian girl's death."

"Okay, okay," said Huanca mildly. "Let it go at that. Let's get to the point. I told you," he went on, looking straight at Benites, "the priests and doctors are also enemies of the Indians and workers. What happened that time in Colca? The subprefect, the doctor, the judge of the claims court, the mayor and the sergeant, the landowner Iglesias, and the soldiers—between them, they caused the deaths of more than fifteen poor Indians. One-eyed Ortega was the worst, the cruelest. And Father Velarde? Wasn't he with the rest of them, running through the streets, waving a pistol and firing at innocent Indians? And García the schoolmaster?"

The timekeeper, his face burning with rancor, paced restlessly up and down. Leónidas Benites listened to Huanca with a hangdog expression, as if torn by deep internal conflicts. The blacksmith's charges stirred a painful uncertainty in his heart. Benites at bottom believed absolutely in the doctrine that says it is the intellectuals who ought to lead and govern

the Indians and the working class. He had learned this in
school and at the university and had gone on reading it in
books, magazines and newspapers, both Peruvian and foreign.
Still, on this night, Benites was taking in the quite opposite
doctrine of Servando Huanca with rapt attention, with respect, even with fellow-feeling. Why? The truth was that
Mr. Taik and Mr. Weiss had thrown him out of his surveying
post, and José Marino had broken off their little partnership in
farming and livestock. The truth was that because of these
injuries, Benites now hated the yanqui bosses as much as the
Peruvian ones—the latter incarnate in the persons of the
Marino brothers. But, he told himself earnestly, between re-
senting those people and plotting with Huanca to stir up the
workers against the Mining Society and, what was more serious, to provoke thus a popular uprising against the whole rul-
ing social and economic order, well, there stretched a vast gulf.
And that was not all the blacksmith had in mind! If the blacksmith sought only a wage increase for the peons, better living
quarters, shorter hours with no work at night or on Sundays,
medical care and supplies, compensation for accidents on the
job, schools for the workers' children, a restoration of the Indians' moral dignity, the free exercise of their rights and, finally,
equal justice for great and small, for boss and day-laborer, for
the powerful and the defenseless . . . but that was not all. Servando Huanca even dared to speak of revolution, of overthrow-
ing the millionaires and the great caciques who infest the
government, to put that government in the hands of the workers and peasants, going over the heads of educated and distin-
guished people like the lawyers, engineers, doctors, scientists
and priests! The surveyor simply could not imagine a black-

smith as minister or bishop, professor or pundit, could not imagine seeking an audience with him or serving as his receptionist. No, that went beyond all reason, all seriousness. Let us assume, for example, that many intellectuals are devious exploiters of the people. But for Benites, considering these matters from a strictly scientific and technical point of view, if ideas and men of ideas constitute both the basis and starting point of progress, what could the poor peasants and workers do on that day they made themselves the heads of state? Without ideas, without a program, without consciousness? They would go to pieces. Of this Leónidas Benites was absolutely convinced. And precisely because he was convinced, the surveyor could not understand why he went on listening to and arguing with Huanca, a crazed man in whose eyes he, Benites, appeared as nothing less than the enemy and exploiter of the working class and the peasantry.

"Come, come, Huanca," replied Benites, "don't talk nonsense. We intellectuals are far from being enemies of the working class. On the contrary—I, for example, am the first person to come and talk freely with you, without anyone forcing me to, and I'm even running the risk that the gringos will find out about it and kick me out of Quivilca."

The timekeeper responded vehemently:

"I bet you that if the gringos give you your job back tomorrow, you won't be coming here any more, and if there's a strike, you'll be the first to open fire on the workers!"

"Yes, absolutely!" said Servando Huanca. "We workers shouldn't put our trust in anybody, not in doctors, not in engineers, least of all in priests. They always betray us. We stand alone against the yanquis, against the millionaires and land-owners, against the government, against the businessman, and against all of you intellectuals."

Leónidas Benites felt deeply wounded by the blacksmith's words—wounded, humiliated, and saddened too. And yet, although he rejected most of Huanca's ideas, he felt growing in his soul a mysterious and irresistible sympathy for the whole cause of the poor day-laborers in the mines. He too had seen many abuses, thefts, crimes, all sorts of outrages committed against the Indians by the foreigners, the civil authorities, and the great landlords of Cuzco, Colca, Accoya, Lima and Arequipa. Now he remembered them. Once, on a sugar plantation in a valley near Lima, Benites happened to be taking a walk with a university classmate, the son of the owner of that plantation, who was a senator and a professor of law at the National University. This gentleman, famous throughout the region for his sadistic tyranny over his hired hands, used to get up before dawn to spy on them and catch them in some dereliction. On one of those nocturnal raids on the mill, his son and Leónidas Benites were with him. The mill was humming, grinding up the cane; it was two in the morning. The boss and his young companions slipped stealthily behind the turbines and the great cane-press, walked along the machines stamped W.R.A.E. and went down a narrow stairway to the area of the centrifuges. They stood still in a corner there, where they could observe the workers without being observed. Benites now saw a throng of naked men, wearing nothing but little loin-cloths, scurrying feverishly here and there at the feet of enormous cylinders that made a deafening crash every few seconds. In the suffocating heat, the workers' bodies streamed with sweat and their eyes and faces wore the sallow and agonized grimaces of nightmare.

"What's the temperature in here?" asked Benites.

"Oh, between 120 and 125," the owner said.

"And how many hours straight do these men work?"

"From six in the evening to six in the morning. But they get a bonus."

And tiptoeing sideways toward the naked workmen but staying out of sight, he added,

"One moment. Wait here for me."

The boss moved forward quickly, grabbed a bucket that he found in his path, and filled it with cold water from a pump. What was he going to do? One of the workers, naked and sweaty, was sitting nearby on the edge of a steel slab. Propped on his knees, his sweat-drenched head rested on his arms. He was asleep. Some of the other workers caught sight of the master and, as always, trembled with fear. And at that moment Leónidas Benites, dumbfounded, saw with his own eyes an astonishing scene, brutal, diabolic. The owner tiptoed up to the sleeping worker and abruptly overturned the bucket of cold water on his head.

"Animal!" he shouted as he emptied the bucket. "Lazy pig! You're stealing my time, you thief! Back to work!"

The worker's body shuddered and then sank to the floor, convulsing violently for some time, like a chicken in its death throes. Then he suddenly sat up, staring into emptiness with fixed bloodshot eyes. Coming to but still somewhat confused, he resumed his work.

That same night he died.

Benites remembered all this as in a flash of lightning while Servando Huanca was speaking to him.

"There's only one way that you intellectuals can do something for the oppressed workers, if that's what you really want, to prove to us that you're our comrades and not our enemies. The only thing you can do for us is to do what we tell you, to listen to us, and put yourselves at our command and serve our interests. Nothing else. For now, it's the only way we can understand each other. Later, well, we'll see. Then we'll be working together, in harmony, like true brothers. Choose, Señor Benites, choose!"

The three men sank into a deep silence. The blacksmith and the timekeeper gazed steadily at Benites, waiting for his answer. The surveyor sat there pensive and dispirited. The weight of Huanca's arguments were winning him over. He could barely move. He felt almost overcome, no matter how much he fell short of understanding his stubborn inclination at this moment toward the cause of the Indians. Benites did not realize—he did not want to realize—that if he was now with the two workers in the hut, it was only because he had fallen into disfavor with the yanquis and with Marino Bros. Why had he not taken pity sooner on the sharecroppers and workers, when he was the surveyor of the Mining Society and on friendly terms with Mr. Taik and Mr. Weiss? Classic type of the petit-bourgeois Creole and Peruvian student, given to every form of toadying to the great and powerful, and prey to all the snobberies and timidities of his class, Leónidas Benites, having lost his job at the mines and finding himself under the heels of his bosses and confederates, was utterly demoralized and in deep despair. His misfortune was so complete that he seemed to himself the most miserable and insignificant of men. He spent his days hanging around the workers' encampments and the rocky places of Quivilca, alone and in a daze, each day more filthy, gaunt, and chicken-hearted. He could not sleep nights and often lay in his bed weeping. He was being consumed by a severe nervous breakdown. Sometimes a throng of black thoughts came to him, among them the idea of suicide. For Benites, life without employment and without social status was not worth the trouble of living. His moral temper, his religious mania, his whole life force could be located exactly between a paycheck and a handshake from some captain of commerce. With those two poles of his life lost or missing, his collapse was automatic, dreadful, almost fatal. When he heard about Huanca, who he was and how he had secretly arrived in Quivilca, he experienced a sudden moral shock. Before seeking Huanca out, he was torn apart by the thoughts crowding in on him. From day to day, he veered back and forth between begging the yanquis for mercy and going to see Huanca, until one night, he felt so desperate, so at the end of his rope, that he went off to look for the blacksmith.

For his part, Servando Huanca did not at first want to disclose his real intentions to Benites. The timekeeper had filled Huanca in on the situation of the workers, the bosses and other high officials of the Mining Society, and he had spoken very ill of Leónidas Benites. But the surveyor's anguished and dramatic insistence on being on the side of the peons and especially the fact that he had been fired by the company carried some weight in Huanca's tactical thinking, and he conversed freely with the surveyor. Maybe—the blacksmith thought to himself—maybe this fellow brought with him some privileged information, some secret document or whatever, that might be useful in the struggle, something he had come across and grabbed in the innermost intrigues of the company and its directors.

"In what way can you help us?" Huanca had asked Benites from the first.

"Ah!" the surveyor had answered gravely. "I'll tell you later. But I've got hold of something terrific. I'll tell you one of these days."

Servando Huanca waited anxiously for this promised revelation which was the object of his tenacious and energetic campaign to win the surveyor completely to the cause of the peons. The blacksmith was in a hurry to see things clearly, to get his bearings as soon as possible, to know every weakness in the position of the Mining Society and the gringos, so as to start in without delay on his mission of propaganda and agitation among the masses. On their own impulse, the workers were already beginning to show clear signs of discontent and restiveness. There was no time to lose. Huanca now spoke again to the surveyor, with growing heat:

"Choose! And choose freely and honestly, without kidding yourself. With your eyes wide open. Think about it! You tell me that the thefts and abuses of the Marinos sicken you and enrage you. You've thought it over and you're convinced that the Mining Society has come to Peru for no other reason than to mine our ores and ship them abroad. So then? And you, why did they throw you out of your job? Why? Didn't you do your duty? Didn't you work? What then?"

"Because Taik let himself be swayed by Marino's gossip!" Benites answered in a wild moan. "That's why! Because Marino hates me. Just for that! But I know how to get back at them. I swear, I'll get even!"

Huanca and the timekeeper, impressed by Benites' vindictive oaths, sat there looking at him.

"That's it," said Huanca, "we have to pay them back! We have old scores to settle with the rich for all those injustices. But it can't be done just by talking. We have to act!"

The timekeeper had his own anger to add:

"And me, me! They owe *me* for what they did to Graciela. Ah, those bastards, those gringo sons of bitches!"

The three men were simmering. The atmosphere in the hut was murky, conspiratorial and dramatic. Leónidas Benites went to the door, looked out through a crack, and returned to the others.

"I have just what you need to harass the Mining Society," he said in a low voice. "Mr. Taik is not a yanqui. He's German. I can prove it, I have a letter from his father, written from Hanover. It fell out of his pocket one night at the store when he was drunk."

"That's good," said the blacksmith, "very good. But what counts is that you've decided to join our struggle against the gringos. There's a thousand ways of screwing them! Strikes, for example. Now that you want to help us, and since you yourself came looking for me to talk about this stuff, I'd like to know whether you can help me get the workers on the move."

After a long silence, charged with nervous tension, Benites, overwhelmed by the clear and simple truths of the blacksmith, said warmly,

"All right! I'm with the workers. You can count on me. Mr. Taik's letter is at your disposal."

"Good," declared Huanca. "Tomorrow night, then, I want the drover García, the mechanic Sánchez, and the gringos' houseboy brought here without being told why. And you," he said to Benites, "you bring me Mr. Taik's letter tomorrow. Tomorrow, I think, there'll be six of us. Tonight we start with three—a good number."

A few minutes later, Leónidas Benites left the hut, taking care to stay out of sight. A few minutes after that, Servando Huanca left, taking similar precautions. He cut across to the right, walking slowly and calmly, and disappeared behind a little rise, around Sal Si Puedes. His footsteps quickly faded in the distance.

Inside the hut, the timekeeper latched the door, blew out the lamp, and went to bed. He kept his clothes on as usual because of the cold and the roughness of his pallet. He could not sleep. Among all the words and images he retained from the blacksmith's exhortations, words like *labor, wages, workday, bosses, exploitation, industry, commodities, grievances, class consciousness, revolution, justice, United States, petit-bourgeois, capital, Marx*, and so on, there passed through his mind that night the memory of Graciela, the dead girl. He had loved her very much. The gringos had killed her, they and José Marino and the Commissioner. Remembering her now, the timekeeper began to weep.

Outside, the wind was rising, portending storm.

THE END

Notes

Page 1: state of Cuzco—Peru is divided into twenty-three *departamentos*, which are roughly equivalent to our states. Each department is subdivided into provinces, and each province into districts. The action of the novel takes place in the Department of Cuzco, of which Cuzco the city (ancient center of the Inca empire) is the capital, and in the Province of Calca, of which Calca is the provincial seat. Cuzco and Calca are high in the Andes in southern Peru.

Colca, if not an error by the northerner Vallejo—he might have confused it with the Colca River—is probably his lightly fictive spelling for the actual town and province, just as Quivilca is the novel's name for Quiruvilca, a mining town not far from Vallejo's native city, where he worked for a while in his youth. He takes other liberties with names: the Huayal River, scene of a desperate episode in part 2, is an invention, perhaps a portmanteau of two northern rivers, the Huallaga and the Ucayali.

Page 2: commissioner for the mining district—*Comisario* here means police commissioner. As will be seen, he is a very powerful person; he seems to be more secure and menacing in his authority than the provincial official who is technically his superior.

Some of the names Vallejo assigns to his characters have an almost Dickensian aptness, seeming to signify aspects of their bearers' nature. The police commissioner's name suggests a blow struck with a bucket; the rootless Marinos, who come from the seacoast, are, literally, "sailors"; the name Baldomero Rubio conjures up a blonde emptiness; Mr. Taik is indeed a tycoon; and Machuca suggests a tough guy, a bruiser. (Characters to appear later are also justly named—the rich landowner's name, Iglesias, means

127

churches; Luna is appropriate for the subprefect, with his ignorance and lunacy; and our hero's name, Huanca, sounds somewhat like *huaca,* a Quechua word meaning "shrine" or "local deity," while his Christian name, Servando, suggests service.)

Page 3: the Soras—*Sora* is the name Vallejo has invented for the local tribe of Quechuans (Incans), literally "maize people" or "corn mash people."

Page 8: "What did you say, taita?"—*Taita* has different uses, so it seemed best to leave it untranslated. It is a respectful and homely form of "father" used by children—like "daddy"—and it also means something like "master," as when Indians or campesinos address their superiors, in which case it must be roughly similar to the Russian form of address which is usually rendered as "uncle."

In the case of familiar words like *señor* and *señora,* I have sometimes left them in Spanish and other times translated them in various ways, depending on sense and context. I have consistently retained *yanqui* for Yankee, and not merely for the flavor of the Spanish spelling: one sentence about the Yankees and the Indians demanded a ruthless suppression of American League associations, and other instances had to follow suit.

Page 10: an armful of new potatoes—These are not exactly what we call potatoes, although our potatoes did originate in this very area. *Ollucos* are native tubers, moister than potatoes, with yellowish skin and meat.

"Take four *reales*"—Four *reales* would be worth less than a penny.

Page 13: "these men who face the forests and mesas"—*Jalcas* are the high, cold plateaus of the northern cordillera; I suppose they are similar to what are called *punas* in the south—the desolate, dry, windswept *altiplano,* cut by deep gorges and shadowed by mountains and volcanoes over 20,000 feet above sea level. The average altitude of this intermontane basin is 13,000 feet; Cuzco itself, which is only a few miles from Macchu Picchu, is over 10,000 feet.

Page 22: her voice barely audible—The Spanish reads, *exclamó la señora . . . con voz apenas perceptible*—that is, "the señora exclaimed . . . in a barely audible voice." This is a fairly typical example of the stylistic oversights mentioned in the preface, errors of the sort I have silently amended throughout the book.

Page 30: *La Rosada* is another word I decided to leave in Spanish. It means the Rosy One, which sounds rather formal in English, or Rosy, which sounds too slangy and North American. Graciela's skin is not dark but reddish, an uncommon trait among the Indians and prized as a mark of beauty. Her sisters have the same lucky complexion and are also called *Rosadas*.

Page 31: *Chicha* is a cheap and potent beer made from maize. Brewed by the Incas for ceremonial use, it has been for centuries one of the two readiest means (the other being the coca leaf) of dulling the misery of existence in the Peruvian sierra. The *chicha* referred to here is homemade, as opposed to the fancier commercial products of Lima or Arequipa. Juan de Arona, in his *Diccionario de Peruanismos*, remarks with disgust that, diastase being the principal agent of fermentation, it is not unusual to see the Indians spitting copiously into the mortar in which the corn is being mashed.

A *chichera* is a girl or woman who makes and sells *chicha*.

Page 32: "La Poza"—Spanish for well or watering hole.

Page 33: *Gendarme* is Vallejo's gallicism, not Peruvian usage. The gendarmes are sometimes referred to as *soldados*, which has the sense of officially armed men, not necessarily soldiers. In any case, the local police force here is in some ways like a small band of cavalry, its ranks filled by conscripts and, like almost all police in Peru, controlled by the central government. I have used *gendarme* interchangeably with *soldier* and *trooper*.

Page 36: "Uncle Pepe!"—Pepe is a nickname for José.

Page 39: "The green stuff" (*lo verde*) is a kind of Mickey Finn, concocted out of coca leaves.

Page 47: "employment agency"—*Agencia de enganche* is not the usual term for an employment agency. "Agency of cozenage and intimidation" would be more accurate. It is really a jobshark operation, of the kind that used to be common in California's agricultural valleys (and is still not unheard of), in which labor contractors trick or coerce illiterate campesinos into virtual slavery.

Page 50: The subprefect is the chief officer of the province, as the prefect is of the department or state. Both officials have considerable authority over the police and military forces in their jurisdiction; but it is not clear to me, either from this novel or from other books I have consulted, how that power is divided between the political authorities and the actual commanders of troops, between, for example, Subprefect Luna and Commissioner Baldazari.

Page 51: "those half-breeds"—A *cholo* is, to be precise, the offspring of a
white father and an Indian mother (Vallejo's parents were *cholos* in this sense),
but in actual usage the word refers, like *mestizo*, to any person of mixed white
and Indian blood. Although it might be rendered as "half-breed," the propor-
tion is immaterial; everyone is a *cholo* who is darker than you or whom you
imagine to be darker than you. The word is sometimes neutral, sometimes
affectionate—a husband might call his wife "*cholita*," and Vallejo, writing to
his mother, sometimes referred to himself as her little *cholo*—but most often it
is contemptuous. Although racism in Peru has not been maintained by stat-
ute, as in South Africa or formerly in the United States, it is nevertheless a
very large fact of life, and the hierarchies of race are largely commensurate
with social and economic status. Luna and the Marinos obviously regard the
people they call *cholos* as irremediably inferior.

"Hot devil" outfits—*Diablo-fuerte* is a kind of cloth, made of cotton but
very heavy and durable. Sometimes brightly dyed, it looks rather like cordu-
roy and is used for work clothes. The Marinos, in spite of their metamorphosis into bourgeois merchants, have apparently not lost their old taste in
clothes.

Mollendo is a city on the southern coast of Peru; in the first decades of
this century, it was a busy and vital port, second only to Callao.

All of the Mining Society officials and professional personnel—all the
Peruvians—come from the coastal regions, where people are accustomed to
shoes, cafés, eyeglasses, newspapers, houses with windows and electric light,
all the accoutrements of civilization. The illiterate Indians of the sierra seem
to them almost another species, so vast is the gulf between the two ways of
life.

Four hundred *soles*—The *sol*, the principal unit of currency in Peru, was
worth, in 1914, a couple of cents, meaning that the Marinos had amassed
about eight dollars (although of course eight dollars had more buying power
then than it would today.)

Page 52: name day—If, like most Latins, you are named for a saint, that
Saint's Day is your name day (and often, though not necessarily, your birth-
day).

Page 53: "even the deputy"—Peru had, until the 1968 coup, a bicameral
legislature: a Senate and a Chamber of Deputies. At the time of this novel, a

deputy or a senator would be, without a doubt, a man of wealth and power. Fredrick B. Pike, who is not particularly sympathetic to leftist analysis, writes in his *Modern History of Peru*, "The owners of large sierra estates, unchecked *caciques* of their kingdoms, focused their attention on national politics around the turn of the century and easily arranged to have themselves elected to congress. Once installed therein these landowners, referred to in Peru as *gamonales* [this is Vallejo's usual term for Señor Iglesias], were content to become the bureaucratic puppets of the executive Caesar. Dependent upon the support of these congressmen, the president was not inclined to restrain their powers as absolute *caciques* in the sierra. Thus assured of the tolerant forbearance of the executive, the *gamonales* continued to impose feudal conditions on their laborers and, utilizing semi-legal methods of chicanery as well as force, expanded their rural holdings at the expense of Indian communities."

Page 66: "conscripts"—Military service, then as now, was obligatory for every male Peruvian, although in actual practice, then as now, conscripts were mostly Indians and the poor. Theoretically they would be drafted into the army, the civil guard, or the police, but as Vallejo tells, many were siphoned off, legally or otherwise, to work on the great latifundias or in the foreign-owned mines.

Page 69: serfs—This word has a somewhat medieval ring, but I cannot think of a more accurate one for the economic arrangement Vallejo is describing.

Page 71: "body quota"—*contingente sangre* appears to be a contemptuous euphemism. Literally "blood consignment," I have rendered it by a similar synechdoche.

"They're enlistees."—Vallejo refers to three apparently distinct categories, *conscriptos*, "*socorridos*," and "*enrolados*," the latter two always in quotation marks to signify the transparency of the deceit. As we have seen, the *socorridos*, or "assisted ones," comprise those Indians who for one reason or another have accepted a few coins from some jobshark like Marino and then find themselves bound by law to an indefinite term of labor; the *conscriptos*, of course, are those drafted at random; and the "enrolados" or enlistees, according to the Law of Compulsory Military Service (see page 90), are those who have neglected to enroll themselves (that is, register for the draft) and, in the bizarre logic of the system, are therefore considered to have volunteered. The reality is that the Indians know nothing of any of this and so are easily victimized by an elaborate legal shell-game. Vallejo occasionally forgets the categories and refers to the "enlistees" as conscripts or vice versa.

Page 76: amaranths—I have not been able to discover what *guirnales* are; I suspect that this is a misprint (one of many) and that Vallejo meant *guirnaldas*, globe amaranths.

Page 82: If we should be puzzled by these graphic scenes of violence, wondering how the troopers can so brutalize their captives as to render them useless to the bosses, we might recall the treatment meted out by the officers and crews of the slave ships, which sometimes lost half of their cargo before arriving in the Americas.

Page 94: the governor—The *gobernador* is merely the chief official of the district, an administrative subdivision that plays no role in the events of the novel.

Page 103: marineras—The *marinera* is a lively dance of African origin, a sailor's dance as the name suggests.

Page 105: "An ataque"—*Un 'ataque'* must be the Castilian version of the Quechuan word *taqui*, a fast dance or dance tune.

Page 107: "transferred from Colca"—Cannas is the name that appears in the text and is either an error or a mystery. Quite clearly Luna is stationed in Colca (or Calca), the provincial capital. The reader may recall that Cannas was mentioned earlier as the site of the typhoid epidemic that killed two of Braulio Conchucos' brothers, in which case it would probably be a hard day's journey from Colca.

Page 109: In order to avoid chance encounters—As far as I can see, this appropriation of twenty prisoners was not illegal, although the line between the legal and illegal in the exploitation of Indians is thin and blurred. The secrecy is the result of Luna's anxiety in the face of competing demands; he is afraid of Iglesias, not the law—he *is* the law.

Page 111: *Sal si puedes*—literally "Get out if you can"—is a generic name for any place where life is desperately poor, dangerous, and short. Hell's Kitchen would be an excellent equivalent if it were not quite so New York.

Variedades was a big magazine, published in Lima, which contained, as the name implies, a variety of features, from social news and photos to serious fiction and criticism. During his years in Paris, Vallejo contributed a few articles and was for a while a weekly columnist.

Page 113: *El Comercio* is the name of Peru's oldest and best-known newspaper, published in Lima, of course, but during the early years of the century a newspaper of the same name came out of Cuzco, and it is most likely this local paper that Benites has been reading. An issue of the Lima paper would have been weeks, perhaps months, old.

Page 115: "clever young fellows"—A "*señorito* is, literally, a young gentleman, but the diminutive has a rich lexical force for which there is no exact equivalent in English. It refers to a young man given to idleness and pleasure-seeking, with enough money to be safe from the necessity of labor. We might call such a person a playboy if he were rich and well-traveled, but "playboy" is not sufficiently pejorative. *Señorito* is almost always used bitterly or contemptuously and suggests a certain deficiency of manhood.

Page 119: W.R.A.E.—These four letters appear in the Spanish text in lowercase italics. My guess is that they are a trademark, either English or North American, since almost all Peruvian machinery was imported.

Page 121: creole—*Criollo* can have several meanings. For a long time, Creoles were simply those Spaniards born in the New World. The word is still used in that sense, but here it probably means only that Benites is from the coast and that his complexion is on the light side.

TUNGSTEN

was composed in 10½ on 13½ Caslon on a Quadex 5000
by BookMasters;
with display type set in Trump Mediaeval Semi-Bold Condensed
by Rochester Mono/Headliners;
printed by sheet-fed offset on 50-pound, acid-free Glatfelter Natural Hi-Bulk,
Smyth-sewn and bound over binder's boards in Holliston Roxite B,
with dust jackets printed in 2 colors,
by Braun-Brumfield, Inc.;
designed by Will Underwood;
and published by
SYRACUSE UNIVERSITY PRESS
SYRACUSE, NEW YORK 13244-5160